Jesus Our Saviour

REFLECTIONS ON THE SUNDAY READINGS
FOR LUKE'S YEAR

the columba press

First published in 2006 by
the columba press
55A Spruce Avenue, Stillorgan Industrial Park,
Blackrock, Co Dublin

Cover by Bill Bolger
Origination by The Columba Press
Printed in Ireland by ColourBooks Ltd, Dublin

ISBN 1 85607 555 9

Table of Contents

Introduction

The gospel of God's saving purpose

By the end of the second century, the two volume work that we know as Luke-Acts was being attributed to Luke the companion of Paul (cf Phlm 24; Col 4:14; 2 Tim 4:11). The 'we sections' in Acts (16:10-17; 20:5-15; 21:1-18; 27:1-28:16) could suggest that the author accompanied Paul on some of his later journeys. Luke begins his gospel by acknowledging his debt to those men and women who were eyewitnesses of the public ministry of Jesus and who became 'servants of the word', preachers and teachers (Lk 1:2). Although Luke may have been an eyewitness of some of Paul's ministry, he was not an eyewitness of the ministry of Jesus. On the basis of the testimony of the eyewitnesses, he decided to make his own contribution to the written tradition about Jesus (1:3). He writes for Theophilus (a name that means 'lover of God'), probably an influential person of high social standing who had become a disciple. Luke directs his gospel to those who, like Theophilus, already believe, who 'have been instructed' (1:4), in order to confirm them in their faith.

A major theme of Luke's gospel is 'the purpose of God' (Lk 7:30; cf Acts 2:23; 5:38; 20:27), succinctly stated by John the Baptist as, 'All flesh shall see the salvation of God' (Lk 3:6). The purpose of God is to bring salvation in all its fullness to all men and women. Luke understands the role of the Holy Spirit as bringing this purpose of God to completion here and now. As one who is conceived by the Spirit and led by the Spirit, Jesus is fully at the service of God's saving purpose. This is why Luke's Jesus often speaks in terms of a 'must'. In his first spoken words of the gospel, the boy Jesus says to his parents, 'Did you not know that I must be about my Father's business?' (Lk 2:49).

God's purpose requires the co-operation of others, people like Mary who gave herself over completely to God's purpose. It will not be accomplished without opposition. Within Luke-Acts, God's purpose comes into conflict with a variety of human purposes (Lk 7:30; 23:50-51). The chief opponent of God's purpose, and of Jesus who serves that purpose, is Satan (4:13; 22:3, 31, 53). Luke's literary work invites its readers to serve the purpose of God by being receptive to the gift of the Holy Spirit which God gives to those who ask for it (11:13).

According to Luke, Jesus began his public ministry by going to his home synagogue in Nazareth and declaring the purpose of his mission (Lk 4:16-18). Luke presents Jesus as quoting a composite text from Isaiah (61:1-2/58:6). These two passages share the word 'release'. Jesus declares that 'today', the day of his ministry, is the time of 'release', the year of the Lord's favour. Such an announcement was, indeed, good news, especially for those who needed release, the group referred to in the text as the poor, the captives, the blind and the oppressed. These are the economically impoverished who live on the margins. Jesus brings them release by restoring them to their rightful place among God's people.

Luke-Acts suggests that this group, to whom Jesus addresses his ministry in a special way, also embraces those who are excluded because of their occupation or lifestyle. The word translated 'release' is translated 'forgiveness' elsewhere (cf Lk 24:47). Jesus brings 'release' by bringing God's 'forgiveness' to those held captive by a way of life not in keeping with God's purpose. Although some of these would have been wealthy, they were impoverished because of their marginalised status. Jesus' ministry of release is directed to all who live on the edge, whether for reasons of economic hardship, physical illness or chosen lifestyle. Luke portrays Jesus going out to those who are outsiders and bringing them the hospitality of God, releasing them from their state of exclusion.

For Luke, this is what it means to say, 'the kingdom of God is at hand'. God's kingdom comes when the excluded become full members of the community. Jesus spends more time at table in this gospel than in any other gospel. In sharing table with all sorts of people Jesus embodies God's hospitality towards 'all flesh'. In Luke's gospel Jesus is put to death because his inclusive vision and practice, which expresses God's purpose, is experienced as disturbing and threatening by some.

Luke's Jesus calls for an eating style that reflects his own, one which expresses the hospitality of God. If God's purpose is to be realised in the present, 'today', this has implications for those of high social status. On one occasion, Jesus says to his wealthy host, 'when you give a banquet, invite the poor, the crippled, the lame, the blind' (14:13). Jesus calls on him to treat as family and friends those he would normally have kept at arm's length. If the privileged do not heed this call, those on the margins, like

Lazarus, will have to wait until the next life before their situation is reversed. Luke describes the early church as faithful 'today' to Jesus' kingdom mission of embodying God's hospitality. 'There was not a needy person among them, for as many as owned lands or houses sold them and brought the proceeds of what was sold' (Acts 4:34).

Luke gives greater prominence to Jesus' journey to Jerusalem than the other evangelists. It occupies ten chapters of his gospel (9:51-19:28). The evangelist opens his journey narrative in solemn tones: 'When the days drew near for him to be taken up, he set his face to go to Jerusalem.' At the end of his journey, Jesus will be 'taken up' to his Father. His journey to Jerusalem is his journey to the Father. He travels it in the service of his Father's purpose. In 13:31-33 Luke captures the resolve of Jesus to persevere with this difficult journey. Some Pharisees approach Jesus and say to him, 'Get away from here, for Herod wants to kill you.' In reply, Jesus says, 'Today, tomorrow, and the next day I must be on my way, because it is impossible for a prophet to be killed outside of Jerusalem.' In the service of God's purpose, Jesus must go to Jerusalem. Whereas Jerusalem was the goal of Jesus' journey, it is the starting point of the church's journey, the goal of which is 'the ends of the earth'. This journey of the church, like that of Jesus, is travelled under the guidance of the Spirit and is at the service of God's saving purpose.

Luke's gospel is the only gospel to begin and end in an atmosphere of prayer. Luke highlights the prayer of Jesus himself. In prayer Jesus continually embraces God's purpose. According to the evangelist, Jesus' own practice of prayer generated a desire to pray in his disciples, 'Lord, teach us to pray' (11:1). There is an abundance of teaching on prayer in this gospel (11:1-13; 18:1-14). It is only in and through prayer that Jesus' followers can hope to be as faithful to God's purpose as Jesus himself was.

First Sunday of Advent

You may have noticed some changes in the church this Sunday. A wreath with candles has appeared in the sanctuary. A certain restraint has entered our liturgy. The colour of vestments is now sombre violet rather than green; the 'Glory to God in the highest' is omitted at the beginning of Mass. The prayers and the readings of the Mass take on a certain character. We hear words like 'longing', 'waiting', 'preparing', 'promise', 'coming'. The short season of Advent has begun. It is a season that invites us to prepare for the feast of Christmas by focusing on what is really important in life.

It is often the case that suffering can lead us to look more deeply than we normally do, prompting us to identify what is really important and what is less significant. Those who have had a close brush with death often say that, afterwards, they look upon life with new eyes. What was once taken for granted now has new value. What once seemed so pressing now seems less important.

In today's gospel reading we hear the Advent call to 'Watch', to 'Stay awake'. The call to watch is a call to pay attention to what is really important. For us as Christians, what is ultimately important is our relationship with the Lord. That relationship is the foundation of all our other relationships. Advent invites us to pay attention to that most important of relationships. The great prayer of Advent is, 'Come, Lord Jesus'. In Advent, we invite the Lord to come into our lives more fully.

Our relationship with the Lord is not a relationship of equals. He alone is Lord. His will always takes priority over our will. We grow in our relationship with the Lord, when we grow in our freedom to do what he wants. St Paul in the second reading today calls on us, 'to make more and more progress in the kind of life that you are meant to live, the life that God wants'. Advent is a season that calls on us to let God be God in our lives, so that what God wants shapes what we do and say. Mary, the great Advent saint, shows us the way. She was truly watchful; she was awake to what God wanted. Her prayer, 'Let it be to me according to your word', captures that spirit of attentiveness to what God wants which the season of Advent puts before us.

The gospel reading speaks of the final coming of the Son of Man. Whether we understand that coming as happening at the end of time or at the end of our lives, we believe that there will be a final coming of the Lord for each of us. It is in the knowledge of that final coming that we pray, 'Come, Lord Jesus.' We pay attention now to the Lord and to what he wants, so that when he comes at the end he will not be a stranger to us. The gospel reading calls on us to 'Stay awake, praying at all times for the strength ... to stand with confidence before the Son of Man.' Prayer is one important way we pay attention to the Lord now, so that we stand with confidence at his final coming. Advent is a season which highlights the importance of prayer in our lives. When we pray, we attend to what is ultimately important, to the Lord, and we leave ourselves open to his will for our lives. Today's responsorial psalm is a true Advent prayer, 'Lord, make me know your ways.' Advent is a time when we express our longing to walk in the Lord's ways.

We are very conscious that so much of what goes on in our world does not correspond to the Lord's ways. The death and destruction that dominates our news bulletins can leave us feeling disturbed. The image in the gospel reading of 'men dying of fear as they await what menaces the world' does not seem too remote from our experience. The reference to 'hearts coarsened with debauchery and drunkenness and the cares of life' has contemporary echoes. We can look at this darker side of existence and be tempted to despair. We can identify some of this darkness in our own lives and get discouraged. Yet, while acknowledging the darker side of life, Advent calls on us to keep our focus on the Lord, trusting that his light is always stronger than the darkness that seems to threaten us. We attend to the Lord, praying 'Come, Lord Jesus,' opening our hearts to the light of his presence. That prayerful attentiveness to the Lord keeps us hopeful in the face of darkness and enables us to become signs of hope for others.

Second Sunday of Advent

Road works seem to be a permanent feature of life in most countries. In the language of the gospel reading, winding ways are straightened and rough roads made smooth. Some major motorways even result in valleys being filled in and hills being laid low. The purpose of this road building work is to enable us to move around more quickly in our cars. Yet, invariably we continue to struggle with traffic congestion.

As well as our roads, our lives can sometimes get congested. We can feel at times that we are at a standstill in life. We may appear to be making little progress, either stuck in something of a rut or going around in circles. Sometimes we may need the likes of a John the Baptist to help us get going in a direction that gives purpose to our lives. In the gospel reading, John the Baptist, in calling on people to repent, was asking them to think about where their lives were going, and to redirect their lives towards God.

In calling on people to turn away from sin and turn towards God, John also reminded them that God was turned towards them and was journeying towards them on a great highway. However, according to John, if God was to enter their lives, they needed to create a space for God, to make way for God, filling the valleys and levelling the hills of the heart, so that God could enter their lives unhindered.

Advent reminds us that the really important journey in life is the Lord's journey towards us. We may not always know where we are going, but the Lord knows where he is going. We are his destination, and he comes to us on a broad highway with no congestion. The Lord comes to us for a purpose, to take us in the direction he desires for us, towards what the second reading calls 'perfect goodness'. The Lord journeys towards us to take us somewhere we could never reach if left to ourselves. St Paul recognises this in the second reading when he says, 'I am quite certain that the one who began this good work in you will see that it is finished.' The Lord comes to us to complete his good work in our lives, to take us on a journey towards goodness, and thereby, life.

In reminding us of the Lord's journey towards us, Advent

calls on us to make a way in our lives for the Lord's coming. There may be valleys and hills in our lives that make it difficult for the Lord to come to us and to accomplish in us what he wants for us. For various reasons, we can keep the Lord at a distance. Like Simon Peter we might be tempted to say, 'Depart from me Lord, for I am a sinful person.' Our realisation that our lives are not all they could be can leave us wanting to keep the Lord somewhat at bay, out of fear of what he might say to us. Yet, Paul reminds us today that the Lord comes not in judgement but in love. He tells the Philippians that he, Paul, loves them as Christ Jesus loves them. The Lord comes to us in love, not to quench the smouldering wick or to crush the bruised reed, but to complete the good work he has begun in us.

Advent invites us to open our lives to the Lord's coming. From time to time a John the Baptist or a Paul can enter our lives and help us to receive the Lord's coming. We need such people on our life's journey, people who see the good in us that we often do not see in ourselves, who 'recognise what is best' in us, in the words of the second reading, who appreciate the good work that the Lord is doing in our lives, even if that good work is far from finished. Those who see us in this way, help us to receive the Lord's coming, and free us to keep going in the direction the Lord wants to take us.

Today we might remember all those people who had a significant influence for good on our own life's journey. We think of parents, grandparents, godparents, teachers, and friends, all who helped to create a way for the Lord to enter our lives, and we thank God for them. In remembering such people this morning, it is also worth reminding ourselves that the Lord calls us in turn to become a John the Baptist or a Paul to those in our own circle of influence. We respond to that calling by recognising what is best in others and by helping them, in turn, to recognise that for themselves.

Third Sunday of Advent

We are now only a little over a week from Christmas day. The run up to Christmas can be a sad time for many people, especially for those who have been recently bereaved. Christmas, with its emphasis on family gatherings and celebration, can be very lonely for those without much family, who may feel that they have little to celebrate.

The emphasis on joy in the readings this Sunday may ring hollow for many people. Zephaniah calls on the people of Jerusalem to 'shout for joy'. Paul tells the Philippians, 'I want you to be happy, always happy.' For many people, however, sadness can be more the norm, and not just in the run up to Christmas. The uncertainty of the times in which we live can leave us feeling very sad. The hurt that people may have experienced in the course of their lives can leave them disheartened. Our failure to be all we know we could be can leave us feeling discouraged.

The temptation to sadness is very real. It can be easier to give in to that temptation than to fight it. We can allow a heaviness of spirit to come upon us, and to impact on those with whom we live. The call of today's readings is one that we may need to hear, even if our initial reaction to it may be negative. Paul calls on the Philippians to be 'happy in the Lord'. The happiness he refers to is the fruit of our relationship with the Lord. This is not a naïve kind of happiness that is blissfully unaware of the darker side of life. Indeed, when Paul wrote to the Philippians he was having a very difficult time. He was writing from prison, aware that he could be executed at any moment. Objectively speaking, he had many reasons to be sad and discouraged.

This is why Paul's own joy, and his encouragement to the church in Philippi to be joyful, is so striking. The source of Paul's joy is his realisation that, in the words of the second reading, 'The Lord is very near.' This is also the reason why Zephaniah in the first reading called on the people of Jerusalem to rejoice, 'The Lord is in your midst.' The Lord of life is always near to us, especially during those times when we are on the way of the cross. As believers we always live our lives 'in the Lord', as Paul puts it. The Lord is near to us as one who has triumphed over death and who is always at work bringing new life out of our various deaths. The Lord's power at work among us can do immeasurably more than all we can hope for or imagine. This is why Paul can write towards the end of this letter from prison, 'I can do all things through him who gives me strength'. We can each make our own those words of Paul.

Paul reminds us that even when, from a human perspective, we may have many reasons to be sad, the power of the Lord's risen life is at work within us, and in opening ourselves to that power, we can experience a joy that the world cannot give. Prayer is a privileged time for opening ourselves to the power of the risen Lord. Paul says in our reading this morning, 'If there is anything you need pray for it.' What do we need? We certainly need the Lord, and that is why the Advent prayer, 'Come, Lord Jesus,' is so much to the point. A related prayer would be, 'Come Holy Spirit.' In and through these simple prayers of petition, we open our lives to the power of the risen Lord, that same power that one day will transform our lowly bodies into copies of the Lord's glorious body.

The Lord, the Spirit, whom we invite into our lives, will always prompt us to look beyond ourselves to others. In the gospel reading, when people came up to John the Baptist asking, 'What must we do?' he called on them to relate to others generously and justly. This is the kind of living that leaves us joyful. It is in serving others that we find our joy. When Paul was writing from prison, he was more concerned about the Philippians than about himself. Christmas is a time when we are invited to reach out beyond ourselves to others more than we usually do. The custom of visiting others at this time of year is a form of looking beyond ourselves. We cannot pray 'Come, Lord Jesus' without at the same time inviting the Lord to serve others through us. When we allow the Lord to do that, we will experience the Lord's own joy.

Fourth Sunday of Advent

Christmas day is almost upon us. It is a time of year that affects different people in different ways. Most people, especially children, look forward to it. Some dread it and are glad to see the back of it. It is a time of year that can bring out the best and the worst in people. The gospel reading today highlights one of the good traditions of the Christmas season – the tradition of the visit.

According to the gospel reading, Mary visited her older cousin Elizabeth to be with her in her pregnancy, and stayed with Elizabeth three months. This was a visit that seemed to bring out the best in both women. Because of Mary's visit, Elizabeth was filled with the Holy Spirit and the child in her womb leapt for joy. Mary herself was moved to pray the great prayer that we know as the Magnificat. Both women, the visitor and the visited, were graced by Mary's initiative to make this visit.

The journey and the visit are very much part of our own celebration of Christmas. Some members of your own family may have already arrived to visit you for Christmas after travelling a long journey. Others will be setting out in the next few days and their visit is eagerly anticipated. Our airports, ports, bus and train stations will be very busy places over the next few days. As Mary greeted Elizabeth in the gospel reading and that greeting was joyfully received, so the giving and receiving of greetings will be at the heart of our lives over the coming days. The giving and receiving of gifts is central to how we celebrate Christmas. However, the visit can in some ways be the real gift. Bringing our selves to someone by visiting them can mean more than the particular gift we might bring. The second reading makes that point with reference to our relationship with God. What matters is not the particular gifts we might offer to God, 'the sacrifices, the oblation, the holocausts', but rather the gift that we make of ourselves to God, that finds expression in the statement, 'Here I am! I am coming to do your will.'

In a variety of ways we will say that to each other over the Christmas time, 'Here I am.' We offer ourselves to each other in the form of a visit. Such an offering always awaits a receiving, an acceptance. There is nothing more painful than to make a visit and for that visit to be rejected, to make the statement 'Here I am' and for that statement to be ignored. Christmas not only calls on us to make a visit to others, but to receive the visit that others make to us, even if that visit is experienced as something of a burden. Mary's generous visit in the gospel reading was matched by Elisabeth's generous welcome, a welcome that recognised Mary's worth and that celebrated her goodness. If Mary shows us how to visit, Elizabeth shows us how to receive a visit. We welcome our visitors by recognising the good that is in them, by naming the ways the Lord is working in their lives.

The visit is one important way we make contact with each other and stay in touch with each other. Yet, for a variety of reasons, visits are not always possible even between people who are close, who are family or friends. If a visit is not possible, we have other options open to us. One of the signs of our times is the ease of communication. Alongside the more traditional means of the letter and the phone call, we have the e-mail and the text message and so on. Christmas is very much about people communicating with each other, keeping in touch, making connections. It is a time when people remember each other, and out of that remembering, reach across the miles to each other in whatever form. We can say, 'Here I am' in more than one way.

All this activity of people visiting each other and receiving visits from others gets to the heart of what Christmas is really about. Christmas is a celebration of a visitation, not so much Mary's visit to Elizabeth, but God's visit to us. God's visitation was welcomed and received by shepherds and by kings. Christmas invites us to express our own welcome for the Lord who visits us, saying to him, 'Here I am. I want to do your will,' as Mary responded to the Lord's visit to her with the words, 'Let it be to me according to your word.' One of the ways we welcome the Lord and do his will is by extending a warm welcome to each other in the days ahead.

Christmas: Midnight Mass

Most of us are careful to remember the birthday of those who have become significant for us. Because those people matter to us, the day on which they were born is important to us. Whenever we send a birthday card to such a person, we are saying: 'I am so glad that you were born; your life, your presence is important to me.' For nearly two thousand years, Christians have been celebrating 25 December as the day on which Jesus was born. We gather tonight to celebrate Jesus' birth because his life, death and resurrection have spoken to us in some way, and continue to speak to us. His birth would mean little to us, if he himself and all he stands for had not in some way become important to us.

We are here tonight because we have heard the words addressed to the shepherds in the gospel reading as also addressed to us: 'Today, in the town of David a saviour has been born to you; he is Christ the Lord.' We have come to recognise that the birth of this child two thousand years ago to a young couple from a small town in Palestine has had consequences for us. We have come to appreciate that through this human being God calls out to each of us in a unique way. Jesus was born not just to Mary and Joseph; he was born to us all. This child was God's gift not just to one family but to men and women of every generation, to us who gather here tonight. That gift that God gave us two thousand years ago has never been taken back. The child who was born, who lived into adulthood and was put to death, has been raised from the dead and remains with us today. God continues to hold out to us the gift of his Son, who is now risen Lord. We are offered that gift anew every time we gather to celebrate the Eucharist. On that first Christmas night, the body of Jesus was laid in a manger and wrapped in swaddling clothes. Tonight, the same Jesus is given to us in the Eucharist, under the form of bread and wine. We gather to receive this gift anew.

At Christmas, we gather to celebrate the good news that we are a graced people; God has graced us and continues to grace us with the gift of Jesus, who is Christ the Lord. We do not have to earn this gift. Mary's child, the adult Jesus, the crucified and risen Lord, speaks to us of God's unconditional love. God's Son is given to us by God as light in our darkness, as life in our dying, as strength in our weakness, as mercy in our failure, as hope in our losses, as a sure way in our searching. God gives his Son to us, not because we deserve him, but because we need him, because at the deepest level of our being we long for him.

God's giving never changes. What changes is our readiness to receive God's gift. God does not change; it is we who change. Every Christmas we celebrate the same good news, but each Christmas we who celebrate are different. Since we celebrated Christmas twelve months ago, we have all changed in some way. The circumstances of our lives will have changed. Our relationships will have changed. Some of us may have lost people who were significant for us. Just as our human relationships change, our relationship with God changes too. We can grow more or less receptive to God's gift of his Son. This Christmas feast invites us to be as open to receive God's gift of his Son as the shepherds were on that first Christmas night.

In receiving God's Son, we are called to live as people who have been wonderfully graced by God. God gives us his Son and pours the Spirit of his Son into our hearts to enable us to live as God's sons and daughters. We show that we have received God's gift of his Son when we allow God's Son to live out his life in us. Christ who was born of Mary in Bethlehem wants to be born in all of our lives. We really celebrate Christmas well when we show the face of Christ to each other, when God's love becomes flesh in our lives, as it became flesh in Jesus. When that happens, people who walk in darkness will see a great light. This Christmas night, we remember with gratitude all those who have shown the face of Christ to us. We pray that our own relationship with God's Son would grow and deepen, so that God's love would take flesh in our lives.

Christmas: Day Mass

Many of us will have spent time and energy looking for gifts for people in recent weeks. We headed into the city centre more than once to buy the gifts we wanted for those who matter to us. There can be a great sense of relief when the buying is over and we feel that the job is well done.

Why do we give gifts to each other at Christmas time? We probably feel that it is expected of us. Yet, perhaps at a deeper level, we give gifts because we are aware that at the heart of the feast of Christmas is God's giving. In the words of John's gospel, 'God so loved the world that he gave his only Son.' At Christmas, we celebrate God's gift to us of his Son.

Our giving of gifts at Christmas is always selective. Most of us probably make a short list of those we have to buy for. God's giving is not selective in that way. God gives his Son equally to us all. In the words of today's gospel reading, Jesus, the Word, is the light that enlightens all men and women. Each one of us here is equally graced by the gift of God's Son. Even if we have hesitated to receive this gift in the past, God continues to hold out to us all the gift of his Son. At this time of the year in particular, God is saying to each of us, 'Come and receive.'

The gifts we give at Christmas time make a statement to those who receive our gifts. In a sense, the statement the gift makes is more important than the gift itself. The value of the gift consists not so much in what it cost us financially as in what the gift expresses. In giving a gift to someone we can be saying, 'I love you,' 'I value your friendship,' 'Thank you for your love,' 'I appreciate your presence,' 'I forgive you.' God also speaks to us through the gift of his Son. In the words of the second reading, 'God spoke to our ancestors through the prophets, but in our own time … he has spoken to us through his Son.' Part of what God is saying to us through the gift of his Son is: 'I want you to know me as well as I know you.' In giving us his Son, God became flesh, one like us. We can now say, in the words of the gospel reading, 'We have seen God's glory.' In giving us his Son, God says to us, 'I open my heart to you. Come and see.' We usually only open our heart to those we love. The opening of God's heart through the gift of God's Son speaks loudly of God's love for us.

After the hard work of choosing and purchasing gifts for people, we take them home to wrap them. The whole exercise is only complete when we hand over the gift and the person receives it. The receiving of the gift is a very important part of the exercise. We can feel very hurt if, having gone to the trouble of choosing, purchasing, wrapping the gift, it is received only half-heartedly. Christmas is about receiving as well as giving. It is a feast that calls on us to receive God's gift of his Son and all that this gift expresses. God's gift of his Son was not well received by all. In the words of the gospel reading, 'He came to his own domain, and his own people did not receive him.' Yet, the very next sentence makes a wonderful promise to those who do receive God's gift well. 'To all who did receive him he gave power to become children of God.' As sons and daughters of God, we will one day share fully in God's life.

This Christmas morning we are invited to open our hearts to receive the gift of God's Son. Here is a gift that is 'full of grace and truth'. God wants us all to receive from that fullness. Your presence at Mass, your receiving God's Son in the Eucharist, is a sign of your willingness to receive from the fullness of God's gift. Our readiness to grow in our relationship with God's Son is a further sign that we are receiving God's gift in earnest. We do this when we pay attention to all he said and did, and allow that to influence and to shape all we say and do, when we take God's Son as our way, our truth, and our life. Today's feast calls on us to receive God's gift by committing ourselves again to living as disciples of God's Son. What better Christmas gift could we offer to God than this?

Feast of the Holy Family

One of the most distressing experiences for parents must be when their children get temporarily separated from them. I am sure it can happen easily enough in places like busy shopping centres, especially when the child has got to an age when he or she likes to ramble off. When the child is eventually found, firm words are often spoken by the parent. That kind of tension-filled experience is part of normal family life.

In the gospel reading this morning, Luke describes a similar kind of family experience. Jesus' parents expected him to travel with the extended family. However, the 12 year old had different ideas. Luke suggests that even at the relatively young age of 12, Jesus was more concerned with the expectations of his heavenly Father than with those of his parents. As a result, the one who came to seek out and to find the lost, was himself considered lost by his parents, and was sought for until he was found. In reality, Jesus was not lost. He was where he was supposed to be, and it was his parents who ended up somewhat lost as they tried to come to terms with his words, 'Did you not know that I must be busy with my Father's affairs?'

The experience of loosing and searching is one that most families struggle with over time. The child who rambles off in the busy shopping centre is only one expression of that experience. The older teenager, the younger adult, can head off in a direction that parents find hard to understand. As a result, parents can struggle with a sense of loss, as their expectations for their son or daughter appear not to materialise. The tensions of family life can also result in family members separating from each other, not only in a geographical sense but sometimes in an emotional sense too. Even in the absence of any major row, the differences in temperament between family members can leave them feeling strangers to each other. It can be quite late in life before there is any true meeting of minds and hearts.

One of the challenges of family life is trying to come to terms with the different paths that family members take in life. When a family member takes a path that is unexpected, it can be tempting to ask them the question that Mary asked Jesus in the gospel reading, 'Why have you done this to us?' It is an understandable question, one that comes out of love and that reveals the pain of love. Yet, it is a question that can also reveal a failure to see a bigger picture, one that is more complex than our particular expectations of the person allow for. There was something much bigger going on in the life of their young son Jesus than Mary and Joseph realised. There was a mystery to her son that Mary would not fully fathom until Pentecost. There is a sense in which that is true of all of us. There is often more going on in the life of a family member than we could ever understand. From our perspective they can seem lost. Yet, in reality, they may be struggling to be true to something very deep in themselves, something of God. Our primary task may not be to find them and to put them right, but to honour whatever is of value in the path they are taking.

Although Mary did not understand the path her son took at the age of 12, the gospel reading says that 'she stored up all these things in her heart'. It was only over time that she came to understand more fully. That is often the way in our own families. What a son or daughter or parent says or does can leave us very perplexed, and even deeply hurt. It is only over time that we can begin to see what was really going on in all that was said and done. Deeper understanding often only comes as a result of the storing up of memories and, perhaps, the sharing of those memories with others, or the bringing of them to prayer. Our deeper understanding can lead us to make a more compassionate response to the family member in question.

Mary and Joseph were faithful to their son Jesus, even though they did not understand him. We are called to be faithful to each other as family members, even when we remain something of an enigma to each other. The second reading speaks of the love the Father has lavished on us by letting us be called God's children. We are called to reveal something of the lavish love of God in the ways we relate to each other within our families.

21

Solemnity of Mary, Mother of God

As we come to the end of one year and approach the beginning of another year, we tend to look back on the year just gone. Various kinds of TV programmes look back on key events in the year, whether it is in the area of current affairs or sports or film. My mother, and my grandmother before her, had a habit of saying, 'Never look back.' The expression, 'never look back', probably reflected the fact that the past was often something of a struggle. The present and the future was what mattered to them much more than the past. There is something to be said for that approach to life. The New Year, therefore, would be more a time for looking forward rather than for looking back.

Psychoanalysts, psychotherapists, counsellors would certainly not hold to the view that never looking back is the best approach to life. An important part of their work consists in helping people to look back over their lives so that they can face and deal with what has never been dealt with. Many people have found that kind of journey back into their lives very liberating, even if very painful at times.

Looking back can also serve us well when what we look back on is something that brought us great joy at the time, or something that gave us food for thought. Parents might look back on the day when their first child was born. This was something to be savoured, an event that had profound implications for their own lives and the lives of others. Here was a joyful, mysterious moment that called out to be remembered and pondered upon.

It is this kind of looking back that is attributed to Mary in today's gospel reading. She had given birth to her child, Jesus, and the shepherds came to tell her all they had seen and heard when they were out with their flocks in the fields. The gospel reading says that 'Mary treasured all these things (that the shepherds told her) and pondered them in her heart.' What the shepherds told her and what Mary treasured and pondered was what the angels had announced to the shepherds, 'Listen, I bring you news of great joy, a joy to be shared by the whole people. Today in the town of David a saviour has been born to you; he is Christ the Lord.' Here indeed was a word that was worth treasuring and pondering over. Mary pondered the words of the shepherds with a view to understanding them better, with the intention of plumbing the depths of what was said to her. This is a form of looking back that is very valid. In the opening chapters of his gospel, Luke presents Mary as a thoughtful, reflective woman. On the occasion when the boy Jesus went missing for several days and his parents eventually found him in the temple, Jesus said to them, 'Why were you searching for me? Did you not know that I must be about my Father's business?' Luke goes on to tell us that 'his mother treasured all these things in her heart'.

In the past few years the Anglican-Roman Catholic International Commission published an important agreed statement on Our Lady. The statement said of Mary that 'She looked beneath the surface of events.' One good reason for looking back at times is to look beneath the surface of events. We look back to grasp more fully the meaning of what happened for us or to us. As believers, we do this in the Lord's presence, inviting him to journey back with us and to help us to draw life from some moment of grace that he has given us. This is what we might call a contemplative approach to life. It is one that Mary embodies and encourages us to strive towards.

The pace of life today can work against such a contemplative stance. We can find ourselves doing a lot and pondering very little. As a result, we live more on the surface of life rather than pausing to look beneath the surface. At Christmas we celebrate the good news that the Word became flesh. Human flesh, human life, is shot through with the presence of God. There is a divine depth to life that calls out to us. St Paul, in today's second reading, tells us that the divine Spirit is constantly crying out 'Abba, Father' deep within us. We need a contemplative attitude if we are to hear that Spirit within us, if we are to recognise the Lord when he comes to us in the events of life. On this feast day, we might resolve to grow more into Mary's contemplative stance to life this coming year.

Second Sunday after Christmas

The Angelus is not prayed as much as it used to be. Most of the younger generation would not be familiar with it. I suspect it is not a prayer that is taught much at school. Those of us who learned the Angelus realised that the most important line in that prayer was, 'The Word became flesh and dwelt among us.' It is taken straight from the Prologue of John's gospel which we read this morning.

It is an extraordinary statement. The Word who was God became flesh, became embodied in the same way that we are embodied. This is the core belief of Christianity. In the person of Jesus, God chose to have a human body like yours and mine. No other religion makes such an extraordinary claim.

We connect with each other through our bodies, through our speaking, listening, looking, walking, touching and so on. In becoming flesh, in taking on a human body, God chose to connect with us, to communicate with us, in a daringly new way, through a life that was as fully human as yours and mine. God's new way of relating to us makes it possible for us to relate to God in a new way. God has gone to great lengths to relate to us, and God awaits a similar response from us. If God relates to us through a human life, the life of Jesus, we also relate to God through a human life, our own. How we live in our bodies expresses how we are relating to God. St Paul, in the second reading, speaks of our calling to live through love in God's presence. For him, it is above all how we love that expresses how we are relating to God.

In becoming flesh, God became very vulnerable. The Prologue states that the Word came to his own domain and his own people did not accept him. We know what that statement means. The body of Jesus was nailed to a cross. Those physical wounds of the nails were only the last in a series of wounds that Jesus suffered in the course of his life. Before being nailed to a cross, he had already suffered the emotional wound of being abandoned by those in whom he had invested so much. Our bodies also leave us vulnerable. They carry the truth of all our experience, not only our history of being held and loved, but also the history of our pain. We carry in our body the wounds that our living inevitably inflicts on us. We are unlikely to be healed of all those wounds before we die. We will carry some of them into the next life. In a similar way, Jesus continued to carry the wounds of his passion and death after he rose to a new life. When, as risen Lord, he appeared to his disciples, he said to them, 'Look at my hands and my feet.'

Yet in his risen life, the Lord's wounds, like the rest of his body, were transformed, gloriously changed. His wounded flesh is now glorified. It radiates the glory of God. That destiny of Christ points to all our destinies. We believed that our own wounded bodies will also be gloriously changed, as was Christ's body, even though our limited understanding cannot fully grasp what that will entail. That is why Paul prays at the end of the second reading today that God would enlighten the eyes of our minds so that we can see what hope his call holds out for us.

The body of Jesus revealed something of the glory of God even before his death and rising to new life. As today's gospel puts it, 'The Word was made flesh … and we saw his glory.' There is a sense in which that is true of all of us who have been created in God's image, who have been baptised into Christ. Something of God's glory already shines through us, through our bodies, even in this life, regardless of what physical state we may be in. We are called to recognise the glory of God in ourselves and in each other, even though we are still only on the way to that full and final glorious transformation that Christ now enjoys.

In becoming flesh, God has shown us the value of our human bodies. The Word becoming flesh invites us to value our bodies as much as God does. It calls on us to show the same respect for our own bodies and those of others that God shows. The incarnation commits us to keep on working for the healing of bodies, so that something of that final healing that awaits us in eternity can be experienced and savoured here and now by as many as possible.

Feast of the Epiphany

Men and women have always been fascinated by the night sky with its myriads of stars and planets. Once the Wright brothers took to the air over a hundred years ago, it was only a matter of time before we succeed in landing on some of the planets.

The wise men in our gospel reading today were star gazers. They were closer to modern-day astrologers than astronomers. It is difficult to look up at a brilliantly lit starry sky and not be overawed by the wonder, the beauty and the mystery of the universe. That sense of awe in the face of our ever expanding universe can touch what is deepest and most spiritual within us. We can be opened up to the wonder, not only of creation, but of the creator. As one of the psalms puts it, 'The heavens proclaim the glory of God.' According to our gospel reading, the star gazing of the wise men from the east launched them on a spiritual quest, a search for God's anointed one, a king in whom God was present in a unique way. Their fascination with one particular star brought them west to Jerusalem and eventually to Bethlehem, where they found the one for whom they were searching. Having found him, they worshipped him and left him their gifts, before returning home by another way.

There is something of the searcher in all of us. There is a restlessness in us for what is ultimate and absolute, for what is good and beautiful and true. The busyness of our lives can sometimes cut us off from that restlessness within. We can loose touch with the searcher within ourselves. It often takes a period of enforced inactivity to help us make contact again with the deeper longings within us that get silenced by the pace of life. It was while recovering from the wounds of battle that Ignatius of Loyola began to notice his deepest desires for God, his longing to serve God and to do God's will. When he recovered from his wounds, he set out, like the wise men, by a different way. Sometimes an opportunity for quiet retreat can do the same for us. In a prayerful atmosphere, perhaps with some guidance, we get in touch with the searcher within ourselves again. We begin to attend to the Lord and his call. Having met the Lord anew, we return home again by a different way, somehow changed. A pilgrimage can have the same effect on us. We find ourselves joining a group that are travelling together to some holy place, some place that has been touched in some way by God, by people of God. There, in this special place, something deep within us is stirred. We are helped to see ourselves and others in a different light, in God's light. We are helped to take a different way, a better way.

Today's feast speaks to the searcher in all of us. We are invited to identify with these wise men from the East who invested time, energy and resources in seeking out the one whom God sent to us. Their search was very much in response to God's initiative. They came to Bethlehem because God had already visited that place. God had spoken a word which they were alert enough to hear. Our search is always a response to God's initiative towards us. God seeks us out before we seek out God. Over the Christmas period we have been celebrating the wonderful way God has sought us out in the person of his Son, who took on a human life like yours and mine. God sent his Son to seek out and to save the lost, and that includes all of us. We are already the objects of God's search. God's searching love continues to call out to us, and to draw us. Our search is always only a response to that greater search, the search of a love that is greater than any human love.

Today's feast invites us to pause and allow ourselves to be touched by God's searching love, so that, like the wise men, we can set out on our own search for the Lord who seeks us out. As we set out on that journey, the Lord will provide us with stars to guide us. Those stars will often take the form of people who themselves have been true to their own deepest longings and whose lives are pointing towards God. We need to be alert to the signals the Lord gives us to guide our way towards his great light. As we allow that light to shine on us, we too will find ourselves setting out by a different way, one that corresponds more to the Lord's way.

Feast of the Baptism of the Lord

I have a tin box in the house where I keep important documents. I was going through it the other day and I came across my baptismal certificate. I noticed that I was baptised five days after I was born, which was the norm in those days. I had never really paid any attention to the date of my baptism before. I made a mental note of my baptism date when I looked at the baptismal cert and entered it into my diary. It occurred to me that I might pay a visit to the church of my baptism when my baptism day comes around this year, and just prayerfully call that day to mind.

Our birth day is a day that gets remembered every year. There is something to be said for giving our baptism day a remembrance also. The early Christians paid at least as much attention to the day of Jesus' baptism as they did to the day of his birth. The baptism of Jesus stood out more for the first Christians than his birth. They recognised that the day of Jesus' baptism was a kind of a watershed for him. It was the beginning of his public ministry. This was the day when Jesus began to make an impact. Such was the impact he made that it reverberated down the centuries and has resulted in our being present here today in this church.

If the first Christians remembered the day of Jesus' baptism, they also remembered the day of their own baptism. They looked back on that day as a watershed in their own lives. They thought of their lives in terms of before and after baptism. It is difficult for us to have that same sense of a time before and a time after baptism, because we were all so young when we were baptised. Yet, the significance of our baptism is no less than the significance of the baptism of the early Christians. The same sacrament was celebrated in our case as in theirs.

Indeed, it would not be an exaggeration to say that the day of our baptism was as significant a moment in our lives as the day of Jesus' baptism was in his life. Our baptism day was the day when God said to us what was said to Jesus on his baptism day: 'You are my son/my daughter, the beloved, my favour rests on you.' The same Holy Spirit who came down on Jesus on the day of his baptism came down on us. The second reading today speaks of the kindness and love of God who has so generously poured the Holy Spirit over us through Jesus Christ our saviour. If the baptism of Jesus was a more public event than his birth, likewise our baptism was a more public happening than our birth. We understand more clearly today that the baptism of a boy or a girl or of a man or a woman is not simply a private family event but a public church event. A child is born into a family, but is baptised into a church. When parents bring along a child for baptism, they are making a public statement, one which is of significance for the whole church and, in particular, for the local church. At the very least, it is a source of encouragement to all of us in the family of faith to know that our family is growing, that we are receiving into our community a new member whose future living of the faith has the potential to benefit us all.

I have come to appreciate the day of my baptism much more in recent years. I have no doubt that it was a much more important day than my ordination day. Reflecting on the day of the Lord's baptism can bring home to us the significance of the day of our own baptism. The baptism of Jesus set him on a journey that had consequences which no one at the time could have imagined. In a similar way, our own baptism launched us on a journey in the footsteps of Jesus, a journey towards the Father in the power of the Spirit. In the words of the second reading, our baptism commits us to give up everything that does not lead to God, and to have no ambition except to do good – to do what God wants. Every day we seek to be faithful to that baptismal commitment, trying to discern what path leads us to God and what path does not and, then, taking the one that does. Baptism, properly understood, shapes us for life. When you get a chance, make a note of your baptism day. It is worth remembering it when it comes along.

First Sunday of Lent

We have all experienced testing times in the course of our lives. School and college examinations test our knowledge. Our patience can be tested by someone whom we experience as annoying or troublesome. Our courage can be put to the test by the onset of serious illness. Our integrity can be tested when an opportunity comes along to make easy money at other people's expense. Our fidelity to someone can be tested, when that relationship proves more demanding that we had anticipated. Our faith in God can be put to the test when, finding ourselves in a dark valley, our prayers seem to go unanswered.

Today's gospel reading describes how Jesus endured a very difficult test immediately after his baptism. His very baptismal identity was put to the test. Who he was and what his life was about was at issue. Will he use his power to satisfy his own physical appetites or will he use it to serve others? Will he compromise on his worship of God so as to gain worldly power and honours for himself? Will he take the short cut to gaining followers by relying on spectacular stunts, thereby putting God to the test? Jesus came through that testing time because he did not face it alone. God was with him in the test. He was supported by the word of God, and he was strengthened by the Spirit of God, whom he had received at his baptism. In the wilderness of temptation, he remained true to his baptismal identity.

Like Jesus, we have all been baptised and have received the Holy Spirit at our baptism, as he did. Our own baptismal identity will certainly be put to the test from time to time, as his was. Our baptism has made us sons and daughters of God, brothers and sisters of Christ, temples of the Holy Spirit, members of Christ's body the church. Because of our baptism, we have a certain set of beliefs. In the words of today's second reading, we believe in our hearts that God raised Jesus from the dead; we confess with our lips that Jesus is Lord. Who we are as baptised Christians and what we believe will often be put to the test. We may not be led into the physical wilderness as Jesus was after his baptism, but the world in which we live can be experienced as something of a wilderness when it comes to living out our baptism and being true to our baptismal identity. We often experience pressure from our culture to be someone other than what our baptism calls us to be. As Jesus was tempted to take various paths that were contrary to what God wanted for him, we will be tempted in a similar way. As his faithfulness to God's call was severely tested, so also will our faithfulness be tested.

We are at the beginning of the seven week season of Lent. Lent is a season when we face the reality that our baptismal identity is always being put to the test. If remaining faithful to his baptism was a struggle for Jesus, it will certainly be a struggle for us. You could say that Lent is a season when we look temptation in the eye, when we try to identify the particular ways in which we are being pulled away from the path the Lord is asking us to take. It is a season when we try to grow in our freedom to say 'no' to the subtle, and not-so-subtle, seductions of every day living. It is a time when we take an honest look at ourselves, and at the direction our lives are taking. This is not something we can do overnight. The season of Lent is nearly seven weeks long. We are given time, because when it comes to getting the basics right, like who we want to be and how we want to live, we need time.

The same resources that were available to Jesus in the wilderness are available to us as we enter this Lenten time. When Jesus was tempted, he fell back on the word of God to help him through. That same word of God has been given to us as a resource in coping with the various assaults on our baptismal identity. Lent is a good time to make greater use of that resource. Perhaps one Lenten exercise we might consider is to read the readings of the previous Sunday in a prayerful way for a few minutes each day, inviting the Lord to speak to us through them. As we begin our Lenten journey together, we ask the Lord to help us to travel it well, so that when Easter comes we can wholeheartedly renew our baptismal promises together.

Second Sunday of Lent

I watched an interesting programme on Michelangelo recently. It showed how he worked to transfigure a huge block of marble into a beautiful work of art. It is easy to forget that his wonderful David in Florence and his powerful Pieta in Rome were once rough blocks of marble cut out of the mountainside. In a similar way, a painter takes a blank canvas and transfigures it into an image that people delight in looking at. Or a writer takes blank pages and transfigures them into something engaging and absorbing to read.

It is not only marble, canvas and paper that can be transfigured. People can be transfigured. You may have noticed people at airports waiting to greet a loved one. They search each face as the passengers come through the arrival doors. When they recognise their loved one, their faces light up. In a sense, they become transfigured.

We have all had our transfiguration moments. Such moments will often be times when we hear our name spoken in love, when we have a deep sense that we are accepted and valued by someone. We find it easy to remember those moments. In more difficult times we can find ourselves going back to such moments in memory and continuing to draw life from them. Such experiences live on in our memories, and can sustain us long after they have happened.

The gospel reading describes a moment in the life of Jesus when he was transfigured. We are told that, while he was at prayer, 'the aspect of his face was changed'. Not only his face but his whole being lit up; he was glorified. Jesus was transfigured because, in prayer, he heard God his Father call his name in love. 'This is my Son, the Chosen One.' The gospel reading says that Moses and Elijah were talking with Jesus about his passing, his death. Jesus knew that his leaving this world in death would also be his entry into the hands of his loving Father beyond death. On the mountain, Jesus experienced a love that was faithful enough to carry him through death, and the experience of such a love was transfiguring.

Jesus has called us into the same relationship with God that he has. He has sent his Spirit into our hearts, and that Spirit prompts us to cry out 'Abba, Father' to God as Jesus did. Hopefully there will be moments in our own lives when we experience God as Jesus did on that mountain, in a way that leaves us transfigured in the very depths of our being. Different people can hear God call their name in love in different ways. For some, it might happen in and through some experience of nature. In the first reading, the Lord prompts Abraham to look up to heaven and to count the stars. The sight of the stars deepened Abraham's faith in God's loving purpose for himself and his descendants. The wonder and beauty of nature in all its forms can speak to us of God's abiding love for us. The sense of God saying to us, 'You are my chosen one', can also come through the celebration of the sacraments. God's love can touch us at a very deep level in and through the sacrament of reconciliation or the sacrament of the Eucharist. We can come away from those sacramental moments transfigured in some way. For many of us, God's transforming love is experienced in and through the relationships that matter to us. The experience of a human love that is faithful can be transforming, giving us a foretaste of that moment in eternity when we will experience God's love to the full.

St Paul in the second reading encourages us to look forward to that future moment, when the Lord will transfigure these wretched bodies of ours into copies of his glorious body. We live in hope of that final transfiguration, when we will be conformed to the image of the risen Christ. On the mountain, Jesus gave his disciples a glimpse of their own future destiny. Yet, this was only a glimpse of what would come at the end of life's journey. It was not yet the end. They all had to come down the mountain and face into a difficult journey to Jerusalem. We are familiar with that same journey. We all have to face down the road to our own Jerusalems. We know the way of the cross. Yet, we also know that at the end of our journey there will be a wonderful moment when we will hear God calling our name in love, and we are transfigured. We also believe that along the way we will hear echoes of that loving call of God, if we are attentive.

Third Sunday of Lent

We are all aware of the human capacity to cut other people down. This can take many forms, from the cutting remark to the taking of a human life or, indeed, of human lives on a grand scale.

It is never God's will that people be cut down in this way. In the gospel reading a landowner wanted to cut down a tree that was bearing no fruit. Here was a tree that was taking nutrients from the soil and giving nothing in return. From a merely human perspective, it was reasonable for the landowner to insist on this tree being cut down. Yet, the landowner's servant had the audacity to say, 'Leave it … give me time… who knows what will happen in a year's time.' Jesus expected his listeners to recognise his own voice in the words of that servant. Jesus was not in the business of cutting down, even though he was cut down himself in his prime. On the contrary, his mission was to give people every opportunity to flourish, even when the prospect of that happening seemed remote. Jesus reveals a God who wants people to flourish, to be alive with the fruit of the Holy Spirit, with love, joy, peace, patience, kindness, goodness, faithfulness, gentleness, and self-control. This is what it means to be fully alive, and as one of the early church fathers said, 'The glory of God is the human person fully alive.'

As members of Christ's body, we are called to share in his mission of giving people every opportunity to flourish. Hopefully, we can all identify people in our own lives who helped us to flourish, people who encouraged us when we found ourselves wilting, who challenged us when we were stepping out of line, who went on believing in us even when we were loosing faith in ourselves. We might also have very different memories of people who, in various ways, cut us down, who tended to focus on some weakness in us while ignoring our strengths, who gave up on us when we were still learning, who withheld the support we needed at some vulnerable time in our lives. We can identify those who gave us life and those who took life from us. Both sets of memories can be an incentive to look at our own lives and to ask ourselves, 'Am I in the business of cutting down whatever good is to be found in others, or am I in the business of nurturing it?' This morning's parable suggests that nurturing the good in others can be hard work; it can take a lot of time and patience; the results can initially seem disappointing. Yet, it is very much God's work. God works in a life-giving way through our efforts.

If we are to nurture life in others we need to have an attitude of reverence towards them. In the first reading, when Moses drew near to get a closer look at the strange sight of the bush that was blazing without being burned up, he heard God say to him: 'Come no nearer. Take off your shoes, for the place on which you stand is holy ground.' When we draw near to another human being we are approaching holy ground. Each human being is made in God's image and likeness; every Christian is a member of Christ's body. In particular, God identifies with the most vulnerable in a special way; they have a special place in God's heart. In that first reading, God says to Moses, 'I have seen the miserable state of my people ... I am well aware of their suffering.' God's attentiveness to those who are struggling puts a special onus on us to reverence and to nurture the life of the most vulnerable.

In the gospel reading Jesus acknowledges that tragedies happen. We know that people get cut down in their prime, either by other human beings such as Pilate, in the case mentioned to Jesus in the gospel reading, or because of some accidental event, such as the collapse of a tower, in the case mentioned by Jesus himself. Jesus suggests that such tragedies should prompt us to do some soul searching; they are calls to repentance. We are invited to look at ourselves and to ask ourselves what this tragic event might have to say to us. How might it be challenging us to live more fully as the Lord is calling us to live? In the face of destructive acts we ask ourselves how we can be more effective channels of God's life-giving presence. As we hear of people being cut down, we reflect on how we might give ourselves more fully to the work of building people up, and nurturing all that is good in them.

Fourth Sunday of Lent

Many people have worked hard in recent years to reconcile the two traditions in Northern Ireland. Their efforts have borne some significant success. There are other parts of the world where the work of reconcilers has been equally effective. The case of South Africa comes to mind.

In the second reading this morning, Paul declares that God's work is primarily the work of reconciliation: 'God in Christ was reconciling the world to himself.' In working to reconcile people to himself, God was at the same time working to reconcile people to each other. If the work of God is the work of reconciliation, it is also the case that the work of reconciliation is always the work of God. To be engaged in the work of reconciliation is to be doing God's work. Paul was very conscious that God's reconciling work needed human agents if it was to become effective. He states in that reading, 'God gave us the work of handing on his reconciliation.' We have all been entrusted with God's reconciling work.

Today's readings invite us to ask ourselves, 'To what extent am I engaged in God's work of reconciliation?' I suspect that most of us will have an opportunity from time to time to work for reconciliation between individuals who are estranged. Our own families will often provide us with such an opportunity.

The parable we heard this morning is drawn from family life. It can be heard in many ways. One way of hearing that story is as a call to share in God's work of reconciliation. The main character in the story, the father, is someone who worked hard to bring about reconciliation between his sons and himself, and between the sons themselves. In that sense he is truly a Christ-like figure. Through no fault of his own, the father found himself estranged from his younger son. From the moment the younger son headed off on his reckless journey into personal chaos and break-down, the father was alert to every opportunity for reconciliation. He scanned the horizon for an opening no matter how small. When he spotted his son on the distant horizon one day, the father took his chance with abandon. He ran to embrace his son. When someone comes out to meet us, the journey home is always shorter. The opening that the son gave his father was all that the father needed.

Almost immediately, again through no fault of his own, the father found himself estranged from his elder son. For a second time, he headed out from his house to an estranged son. In spite of the elder son's insulting speech, the father addressed him tenderly as 'my son' and spoke the language of communion to him, 'You are with me always.' He was determined to build a bridge to his estranged son. He also tried to build a bridge between his elder son and that son's younger brother, 'Your brother here was dead and has come to life.' We are given a picture of a man working hard to hold the family together. The father in this family is indeed a reconciler, an image of the God who in Christ was reconciling people to himself and to each other.

The portrait of the father in this family may be considered exceptional. Yet, that kind of person is not totally unfamiliar to us either. Many a parent has worked hard to hold a family together. We can probably identify such people in our own experience, people who kept lines of communication open to those who were intent on cutting themselves off from everyone. If lines of communication are kept open long enough, it often happens that those who are estranged eventually travel down them. In the parable, Jesus portrays God's way of relating, and challenges us to relate to each other in the same way. We give thanks to God today for those people in our families, our communities, our country who are relating in this way – the reconcilers, the bridge builders, those who are prepared to move from where they are to make the journey shorter for others. We also know all too well that there are other people who are intent on dividing. This is why we each need to seize whatever opportunity the Lord gives us to share in his reconciling work.

Like the father in the parable, we are called to scan the horizon, to be on the look out for those who, like the younger son, are slowly struggling towards us. Like that father we are called to go out to those who, like the elder son, are frozen with anger and appear to be going nowhere. Whenever we respond to that call, God's reconciling work in Christ is being brought to completion through us.

Fifth Sunday of Lent

An issue that society constantly has to face is how best to deal with moral failure. It is not just an issue for society at large. It is an issue for each of us as individuals, for the families and the communities to which we belong. How do I deal with moral failure in myself and in others? How do we together deal with moral failure among us? There are no simple answers to those questions. The temptation can be to settle for simple answers.

In the gospel reading, the men who brought an adulterous woman to Jesus were suggesting a simple answer to her moral failure. Condemn her to death by stoning. Remove the sinner from the community so that no trace remains. That particular approach to moral failure is not peculiar to the time of Jesus. Every generation has its own version of it. Most democratic countries may have removed capital punishment from the statute books, but we have other ways of eliminating people. The call to lock someone up and throw away the key could be understood as a more refined form of eliminating someone by stoning. Take them out of circulation; hide them away. We can eliminate people in other, more subtle ways. We might think of the relative that never gets spoken about because he or she has done something that embarrassed the family. Whole groups can get written out of the story of a people, because they were perceived not to measure up in some way to what was expected.

The gospel reading makes clear that this is not Jesus' way of dealing with moral failure. He could not agree with the religious leaders that, in the case of this woman, the Law of Moses should take its course. He understood that the situation was far more complex that their simplistic solution allowed for. The religious leaders saw the issue very simply: they were good; she was bad; the bad needed to be eliminated to protect the good. There is a primitive logic at work here into which people can slip from time to time. Jesus was reluctant to engage these men in conversation at all, but when he did speak, his brief comment cut through their simplistic analysis and showed it up in all its inadequacy, 'Let him who is without sin cast the first stone.' Jesus was reminding them that the sin which they so despised in the woman was alive and well in themselves. They could not look at her without looking at themselves, and if they looked honestly at themselves their attitude to the woman would have to change. The slow procession of men away from the woman and from Jesus does them some credit. It indicates that there was some openness in them to the truth contained in what Jesus said.

Jesus did not deny that the woman had sinned, but he strongly denied that her sin made her any different from anyone else, including those who regarded themselves as virtuous. The gospel reading this morning does not encourage us to deny the reality of sin in ourselves or in others, but it does assure us that when we bring our sin to the Lord we will not hear a word of condemnation. The Lord does not deal with sin by eliminating the sinner. St Paul knew that. Before Paul met Christ, he would have been comfortable in the company of those men who brought the woman to Jesus. However, his meeting with the risen Lord made him a much humbler man. As he writes in today's second reading: 'Not that I have become perfect yet ... I am still running, trying to capture the prize for which Christ Jesus captured me.' He knew from his own experience that the Lord did not deal with sin by eliminating the sinner. Far from eliminating sinners, Christ allowed himself to be eliminated for the sake of sinners.

The men who brought the woman to Jesus saw her only in terms of her past, while being blind to their own past. Jesus' way of looking at her was far more generous: he saw the whole picture of her life, not just one little bit of it. Seeing the whole picture of her life, he also saw that she had a future, which those who brought her to Jesus would have denied her. When the Lord looks at us he sees the full story of our lives, not just a couple of lines of our story. The Lord knows that our story is unfinished, and will only be complete when he comes to transfigure our lowly bodies into copies of his glorious body. The first reading assures us that the Lord is always doing a new deed in our lives, constantly creating us anew.

Palm Sunday

Some of us may have accompanied loved ones on their last journey, as they passed from this life to the next. The stages of the final journey of a loved one can remain etched in our memories. Their journey was, in a sense, our journey. We travelled it with them. Very often, it is only some time after the death of our loved one that the true significance of that final journey becomes clear to us. We come to see it in a new light; we come to understand what was going on in a way that was not possible at the time.

The final journey of Jesus was etched in the memory of his disciples. They too came to understand the full significance of that final journey only afterwards, in the light of Easter and with the coming of the Spirit. What they initially regarded as a great tragedy came to be seen as good news. A story of brokenness and failure came to be recognised as a story full of promise and hope. That is how we read and listen to Luke's story of Jesus' last journey this Palm Sunday. We hear this story, not as a depressing word, but as a word that nourishes us and strengthens our faith and hope.

Luke emphasises that Jesus died as he lived. He lived prayerfully and he died prayerfully, praying to God that Simon's faith would not fail, praying for forgiveness for his executioners, praying that his Father's will would be done in his life and, with his final breath, praying himself into the welcoming hands of his Father. Jesus lived compassionately and he died compassionately, healing the wounded ear of one of his enemies, granting Peter a look of acceptance at the very moment when Peter denied him, promising Paradise to the condemned man who turned to him in his hour of need. The experience of his passion and death did not change Jesus. He remained the same person during his passion and death as he was during his public life, a person in prayerful communion with God and in compassionate communion with all men and women, including those who rejected him and failed him.

The Jesus who lived and died is also the Jesus who is risen. As risen Lord, he remains in prayerful communion with God, interceding for us, and he remains in compassionate communion with ourselves. He joins us on our own life's journey, as he joined the two sorrowful disciples on the road to Emmaus. As the Lord journeys with us, he pours out his Spirit into our hearts, so that we can journey in the same prayerful and compassionate way that he journeyed. His Spirit enables us to be prayerful and compassionate people as he was, in good times and in bad, when the path of life is easy and effortless and when it is painful and difficult. The portrait of Jesus that Luke gives us in his passion story is also intended as our portrait. We are being invited to identify with Jesus, to follow him, to become, with the help of the Holy Spirit, the person he was and is.

As we listen to Luke's passion story we might find it easier to identify with the other characters in the story than with Jesus. We might recognise something of ourselves in the disciples who, at the last supper, argued as to which of them was the greatest, in the followers of Jesus who, at the moment of his arrest, resorted to physical force when a different response was called for, in Peter who lacked the courage of his convictions under pressure. We might even recognise something of ourselves in Judas who turned a sign of affection into a signal of betrayal. I suspect many of us could also recognise something of ourselves in those who responded well, in Simon who helped to carry Jesus' burden, in the good thief who confessed his sin and turned to Jesus in trusting prayer, in the centurion who saw more deeply than any other person present on Calvary, in Joseph of Arimathea who did not go along with his peers in the Jewish council but stood apart. Wherever we locate ourselves in the story, the prayerful and compassionate Saviour opens his arms to receive us and to empower us. That is why this story is good news for us all.

Holy Thursday

When Jesus washed the feet of his disciples, he was serving them in a very simple but very loving way. The service that Jesus performed for them on Holy Thursday was only a sign of a much greater service that he would perform for the disciples and for all of us on the following day. On Thursday he laid down his garments to wash his disciples' feet. On Friday he would lay down his life for them and for all of us gathered here this evening. Jesus spoke of himself as the one who came not to be served but to serve and to give his life for many.

Our calling as followers of Jesus is to love one another as he has loved us, to serve one another as he has served us. We are called to be Holy Thursday people, people who stand ready to serve one another. Parents who have brought their children here to this Mass are Holy Thursday people, because they serve their children every day. In a sense, children make servants of us all, but, in particular, of their parents. Parents care for their children in a whole variety of ways every day, seeing to it that they are washed, clothed, fed and provided for. This is the service that Holy Thursday celebrates and honours. When children become adults they often find themselves caring in various ways for their parents. Our parents, who spend so long caring for us, often come to need our care when they become old and infirm. The care that adult men and women give to their parents is an-other expression of the service that Holy Thursday celebrates and honours. The family is the basic context in which we live out the Lord's call, in today's gospel reading, to wash each other's feet, to serve one another as he has served us.

There are all kinds of other services that people render out-side the context of their families. We might think of those who provide opportunities for children to be engaged in various sporting activities. So often, the running of football clubs and other sports clubs is dependant on people who are prepared to give their time and energy to train youngsters, to referee matches, to organise competitions and so on. Service, in the strict sense, is work done on behalf of others without looking for any financial reward. Thankfully there are many people in our communities who are still willing to serve in that sense.

We might think this Holy Thursday of all those people who serve in a variety of ways in our local parish. The family Mass group who put time and energy into children's liturgies are true servants in that gospel sense. There are others who ensure that the older people of our community are given opportunities to live life to the full, and to continue to develop their gifts and talents. Many other parishioners offer their services as readers, as Eucharistic ministers, as collectors, as members of the choir, the baptism team, the liturgy group, the communications group, the parish pastoral council and so on. We sometimes take our servants for granted because they are always there, just as when we were children we often took our parents for granted. Holy Thursday is a good day on which to remember all our servants, and to thank God for them.

In today's gospel reading, Peter resisted the service that Jesus wanted to perform for him. Peter said to Jesus, 'Never! You shall never wash my feet.' He tried to prevent Jesus from serving him. Sometimes we too can block people from serving us. Perhaps we feel that we can manage best on our own. Yet, in reality, whereas we all have something to give to others, we all have something to receive from others also. We all need each other's gifts and service. We are called both to serve others and to receive the service of others. On this Holy Thursday we pray not only for the willingness to serve but also for the openness to receive the service that the Lord wants to offer us through the members of his body.

Very shortly we will be invited to the altar to receive the Lord in the Eucharist. The Lord, who washed the feet of his disciples at the last supper, also gave them the gift of himself under the form of bread and wine. The Lord continues to give us that same gift of himself in the Eucharist this evening. The Lord's gift of himself in the Eucharist is a privileged way in which he continues to serve us today. We need this particular service that the Lord offers us through the Eucharist if we are to become the servants he is calling us all to be.

Good Friday

This is probably one of the only days of the year when we gather in numbers in the church at 3.00 pm in the afternoon. We gather at this particular hour in memory of Jesus who was crucified at this hour. Crucifixion was a particularly degrading and cruel form of Roman execution. For anyone to die in this way, on a Roman cross, is a tragedy, regardless of what wrong they may have done. For an innocent man to be put to death in this way is an outrage.

In that sense, the story we have just heard from John's gospel could hardly be described as good news. The unjust condemnation to a cruel death of someone who stood in a special relationship with God and whose whole life was lived in service of others is surely bad news. Indeed, most of the human characters in the story we have just heard have little to recommend them: Judas who betrays Jesus in secret; Peter, the leading disciple, who denies Jesus in public; the high priest who led the effort to have Jesus put to death, Pilate who hands over a man for crucifixion that he had publicly declared to be innocent. Yet, the better side of human nature is also represented there: the mother of Jesus and the beloved disciple who stood when others ran; Joseph and Nicodemus who saw to it that, if Jesus could not have a dignified death, he would at least have a dignified burial. These are the shafts of light in the darkness. Towering above even these good people, however, there is Jesus himself, the light of the world. It is above all because of him that the grim story we have just heard is indeed good news; it is because of him that the awful events of Golgotha have come to be known among us as Good Friday.

The passion and death of Jesus is good news because there is much more going on here than just the tragic execution of an innocent man. In John's gospel Jesus says to Pilate that he came into the world to bear witness to the truth, in other words, to reveal God to us. The God he reveals to us is a God of love and a God of life. Jesus lived and died to make the God of love and life known to us. It is above all in the hour of his passion and death that Jesus reveals this God of love and life most fully. It is God's giving of his Son, the Son's giving of himself, that reveals God's

44

name to be 'love', and authentic love is always life-giving. In John's gospel the blood and water flowing from the side of Jesus is a symbol of the life-giving power of God's love.

When we read the story of Jesus' passion and death, at a surface level we are aware of the human capacity to inflict death. At a deeper level we recognise God's love and God's desire that we have life and have it to the full. At a surface level we might be repelled by this story. At a deeper level we are drawn to it, and drawn to the God who is revealed by it. Indeed, Jesus says of himself, 'When I am lifted up from the earth, I will draw all people to myself.'

On this Good Friday afternoon we have come to this church because, in some sense, we have been drawn here by the Lord. We will shortly approach to venerate the cross. The central aisle of this church will become the path to Golgotha. We do not approach to venerate an instrument of torture, but to venerate the God of love and life who has been revealed to us in Jesus. The second reading encourages us to approach this 'throne of grace' with confidence, knowing that there we will find mercy and grace.

As we approach the cross, we do so as people who have had our own experiences of the passion that may have left us broken in body, heart or spirit. This Good Friday, we are invited, in the words of John's passion, to 'look on the one whom they have pierced', and to allow the light of God's life-giving love that shines through the cross to envelope us and to renew us. Then we can leave here with a renewed conviction that light shines in our darkness and the darkness does not overcome it.

As we leave here we will have other opportunities to venerate the cross. We continue to 'look on the one whom they have pierced' in the faces of our fellow men and women who suffer and struggle. We continue to venerate the cross whenever we help to carry each other's burdens.

Easter Vigil

It is easy to become disheartened when we look around at our world today. We sense that much of the world has become less safe. Those who deal in death can appear to be gaining the upper hand. We can get discouraged by the violence, the hatred and despair that seem to be very much in evidence. We can easily feel helpless before it all.

The same forces of evil and death, of which we are so aware today, put Jesus on the cross. In raising his Son from death, God was making a powerful statement that evil and death need not have the last word. At least on this one occasion the powers of evil and death did not have their way. God's way prevailed and God had the last word, as he brought his Son through the darkness of death into the light of a new life. God's last word was a word of love. God's love for his Son raised him from the dead; God's love for humanity led God to give his Son back to us, even though he had been crucified by us. In raising his Son from the dead, God sent his Son back into the world that had rejected him. God's persistent and faithful love ensured that the powers of death and darkness would not prevail.

The persistent and faithful love of God that conquered the dark forces of evil and death on that first Easter morning is as real today as it was then. God continues to face down the forces of death and destruction today. When we celebrate Easter we are not simply remembering a victory that belongs to the past. We are celebrating a victory that is ongoing. We are celebrating a Lord, whose loving and life-giving power at work among us is constantly bringing new life out of death, continually transforming our tombs into places of hope. Tonight's feast invites us to look all around us for the signs of that victory in our own lives and in our world today.

Because Easter is a present reality and not just a past event, the Lord calls us to become Easter people. Like the women who came to the tomb on that first Easter morning, we are constantly being sent forth as witnesses to the victory of Easter. As Easter people, our whole approach to life should witness to the Easter truth that love is stronger than hatred, and life is stronger than death. As Easter people, we approach every situation, no matter how threatening or painful it might be, with hope in our hearts, because we know in faith that God, who worked powerfully in the darkness of Golgotha, continues to work in the same life-giving way in all our dark places today. As Easter people we keep on working to ensure that the forces of death and destruction do not have the last word, because we know that this is God's work today, as much as it was two thousand years ago, and we want to align ourselves with that work.

As Easter people, we show the same faithfulness to the broken as God showed to his broken Son. We are alert to the stone rejected by the builders, recognising that it can become a cornerstone. As Easter people, we try not to allow despondency and negativity to take possession of us. When we sense that happening, we invite the risen Lord to join us on the path of life, as he joined the two disciples on the road to Emmaus, and we ask him to pour his Spirit afresh into our hearts and to fan into a living flame once more the gift of Easter hope.

As Easter people we do not get too troubled when our plans fail to work out as we had expected, because we know that God's plan for our lives is always more wonderful than our own plans. When the women came to the tomb on that first Easter morning they planned to anoint the body of Jesus. What they discovered on that Easter morning rendered their spices and their plans redundant. God took them by surprise. They were now into unknown territory. The gospel reading says, 'They did not know what to think.' The familiar, the expected, was shattered, and this was both disconcerting and exciting. We too can discover that our plans are really too small to contain the work that God is doing in our lives. As Paul says to the Corinthians: 'No eye has seen, nor ear heard, nor the human heart conceived, what God has prepared for those who love him.' Easter teaches us to hold our plans lightly, so that we remain open to the surprising new work that the God of life is always doing in our midst.

Easter Sunday

We are all only too well aware of the reality of death. We hear almost every day of those killed on our roads. We are horrified at the number of people who are callously murdered. Some people in this church may have had their own very personal experience of death in the course of last year, with the loss of a loved one. From time to time we are reminded of our own mortality when we brush up against serious illness.

When Mary Magdalene approached the tomb of Jesus on that first Easter morning, she was preoccupied with death. Jesus had been cruelly put to death by the Romans in his prime. She had stood by the cross and watched him die. Now she was approaching the tomb to complete the rituals associated with death. The evangelist says 'it was still dark' when Mary approached the tomb. The darkness of the morning echoed her darkness of spirit. To her amazement she discovered the tomb was empty. This discovery only added to her darkness of spirit. Not only had Jesus been put to death, but his body had been stolen. Her discovery of the empty tomb merely deepened her grief. It was only when the risen Jesus appeared to her and called her by name that she understood why the tomb was empty. The tomb was empty because Jesus had been raised from the dead and was now alive. Filled with new joy, new hope, new energy, she went to the disciples and excitedly declared, 'I have seen the Lord.'

That declaration of Mary Magdalene, 'I have seen the Lord,' is the heart of the Easter message. Jesus who was crucified has been raised by the Father and has been given the name 'Lord' which is above all names. Easter declares that the one we worship is not a dead hero but a living Lord. The good news of Easter is that the tomb of death has been transformed by God into the womb of new life. This took everyone by surprise. The gospel reading suggests that even Peter did not immediately understand the true meaning of the empty tomb. It is only of the beloved disciple that the evangelist says: 'He saw and believed.' He alone understood why the tomb was empty; he alone saw that life had triumphed over death. There will always be some who see more deeply than others.

The feast of Easter is the feast of life. In a culture where death is so dominant, we need to savour this feast of life. At Easter we renew our faith in a living God who transforms death into life. If the death of Jesus reveals a God of love, the resurrection of Jesus reveals a God of life. We know from our own experience that genuine human love is always life-giving, and divine love is profoundly life-giving. At Easter we celebrate not only what the God of life has done for Jesus, but what God can do for us all. Because of Easter, we can face our own personal death with hope. Easter teaches us that the journey to the tomb is not ultimately a journey to death but, rather, as Mary Magdalene discovered, a journey to a wonderful and surprising new life. In the face of death, we too, like her, will discover that 'No eye has seen, nor ear heard, nor the human heart conceived what God has prepared for those who love him.'

If Easter enables us to face our own death with hope, it also encourages us to look at all our other experiences of death with new eyes. There is a sense in which we have to deal with death throughout our lives, long before the moment of our own personal death arrives. At any stage in life we can find ourselves dealing with very significant losses. In such times, Easter, the feast of life, can speak powerfully to us. Because the Lord is risen, we do not face these losses alone. With St Paul, we can say, 'I can do all things through him who strengthens me.' The risen Lord can work powerfully in all our experiences of weakness.

All those to whom the risen Lord appeared were sent out as messengers of Easter hope and joy, as agents of new life. This is the call of Easter and it is addressed to us all. Easter, the feast of life, sends us forth to create a culture of life. We are faithful to that Easter calling whenever we help others to make new beginnings, whenever we work with others to help those who are struggling to live life to the full, whenever we are present to people in ways that enable their gifts to come alive and be placed at the service of others.

Second Sunday of Easter

Large numbers of people are killed or wounded in war zones throughout the world today. Most of us will never have been in a war zone; we never have had to live with the fear of injury and death that being in the midst of a war generates. Yet, we probably have been wounded in one way or another by life. Some of us may carry the marks of physical wounds, resulting from surgery. We look on these wounds as necessary, and ultimately life-giving.

Most of us will carry within us wounds that are not so visible to the naked eye. Whatever about our bodies, our hearts will have been broken. If we have ever loved another human being that will certainly be the case. We cannot go on loving someone without experiencing emotional pain along the way. We generally come to terms with those wounds, accepting them as an integral part of love, indeed as a sign of love. Some of us will also carry emotional wounds suffered at the hands of people we found difficult to love. These emotional wounds can be much harder to come to terms with. We can have painful memories of people who bullied betrayed or ridiculed us. It can be a struggle to forgive such people. We sense that the wounds they inflicted have complicated our relationship with others, including those we love most.

Today is the second Sunday of Easter. There is a strong focus on the risen Jesus in the readings, as we might expect. Yet, the wounds of Jesus, and those of his followers, are also central to today's readings. When the risen Jesus appeared to his disciples, the evangelist tells us that he showed them his hands and his side. When he appeared to them a second time, with Thomas present, he said to Thomas, 'Put your finger here, look, here are my hands. Give me your hand; put it into my side.' The gospel reading today is telling us that the risen Jesus is also the wounded Jesus. Jesus endured the physical wounds of crucifixion. He suffered the emotional wound of being violently rejected by those who saw him as a blasphemer and a disturber of the people. He also endured the emotional wound of being betrayed, denied and abandoned by those who were closest to him and in whom he had invested so much.

When Jesus appeared to his disciples, he appeared to them as the wounded one. Yet, his wounds did not define him; he was more than the wounded one. He was also the risen one. His wounds had been transformed; they now had a new meaning. Whereas a few days earlier, his disciples would have understood Jesus' wounds as signs of defeat and failure, they now came to see his wounds as signs of God's powerful presence. Jesus' wounds now spoke to the disciples of the God of love and life; they spoke of a love that is stronger than sin and of a life that is stronger than death. That is why, according to the gospel reading, when the disciples saw the Lord's wounds, they were filled with joy, and why Thomas, on seeing the wounds of Jesus, exclaimed, 'My Lord and my God.'

In the gospel reading, the disciples to whom Jesus appeared were themselves deeply wounded. They had locked themselves in a room for protection, paralysed by fear. Recent events in Jerusalem had left them battered and bruised. They were grieving the loss of the one who had given meaning to their lives; they were struggling to come to terms with their own failure to stand by him when the test came. When the risen Lord appeared to his wounded disciples, he breathed the Spirit of God's love and life into their wounds. From that moment on, they were no longer paralysed by their wounds. Rather, they became channels of the Lord's life to others, as shown by the first reading.

The Lord who came to his wounded disciples also comes to us in our own wounded condition. Like them, we may be burdened by a sense of our own failures, or we may be grieving the loss of someone who has given meaning to our lives. Yet, we believe that the wounded and risen Lord, who stood among his disciples on that first Easter morning, also stands among us. We trust that he can do for us what he did for his first disciples. We look to him to breathe his life-giving Spirit into our hearts, to enable us to minister to others, in spite of our wounds. Indeed, the Lord can work powerfully through our wounds in the service of others. We ask the Living One to transform our wounds into channels of his life-giving presence to others.

Third Sunday of Easter

As the days get longer, many of us are more inclined to get out and to do more walking. We walk where we choose to walk, and we choose some route because we know we will like it. In a broader sense, we tend to take certain paths in life because we are attracted to them. We choose to take one path rather than another because we sense that this is a path that would suit us.

However, there are times when, in the words of Jesus to Peter in today's gospel reading, we find ourselves being taken where we would rather not go. Jesus identifies this moment in Peter's life with his growing older. As we get older we are often taken where we would rather not go, because of failing health.

Even before we grow old, we can find ourselves taken where we would rather not go. At the beginning of the gospel reading, we find the relatively young Peter in such a place. Jesus, who had been at the centre of Peter's life for some time, had been put to death. The journey on which Peter had set out with such enthusiasm had come to a painful end. Peter had given up his fishing to follow Jesus. He now found himself going back to his fishing, going where he would rather not have gone. In going back there, he seemed to have lost his touch. In spite of working all night, he and his companions caught nothing.

We might be able to think of times in our own lives when we found ourselves being taken where we would rather not go, times when we felt as if we were going backwards rather than forwards, when nothing we put our hand to seemed to work out – like fishermen, fishing all night and catching nothing. At such times, we can get very disheartened. We can find ourselves wondering if we have the energy to keep going.

Yet, the gospel reading this morning assures us that in such moments the Lord is very near to us. Even though the shore of the Sea of Galilee must have seemed very bleak to Peter and the others that morning, Jesus came and stood on that shore. The Lord came to them and met them in the ordinary circumstances of their day-to-day lives, at a time when they were at their lowest ebb. The Lord relates to all of us in the same way. When we find ourselves being taken where we would rather not go, the Lord comes with us. No matter how bleak the shore of our lives may seem, we can be assured that he is standing there. We may not recognise him. It might take another disciple to point him out to us. But he is certainly there.

On that early morning by the Sea of Galilee, the Lord's presence took a number of forms. It first took the form of a call to head out again after failure. 'Throw the net out to starboard and you will catch something.' In our own dark moments, the Lord is present in those who encourage us to head out again, inviting us, perhaps, to take a slightly different direction, starboard rather than port. When we appear to have reached a dead end, we need people who can see life teeming beneath the surface that we might be blind to, people whose hopeful vision does not allow us to throw in the towel.

The Lord's presence on that early morning by the Sea of Galilee also took the form of an offer of hospitality, 'Come and have breakfast.' In those times when we are brought where we would rather not go, the Lord comes to us in those who are hospitable towards us, who are willing to share their table and something of their lives with us. The fare they put before us can be simple, as simple as bread and fish, but the impact on our lives of their hospitality can be profound. They provide a space where we can be restored. They engage in the mission that Jesus gave to Peter when he said to him, 'Feed my sheep.' We are all called to reveal the Lord's nurturing presence to each other.

According to the evangelist, when Jesus told Peter that one day he would be taken where he would rather not go, Jesus was talking about Peter's death. Very few of us want to die, I suspect. We fight against being brought where we would rather not go. Yet, our faith assures us that the Lord will be standing on that particular shore too. In death we will encounter the same risen Lord that Peter and the others met on the shore of the Sea of Galilee.

Fourth Sunday of Easter

Some of us find it difficult to get up in the morning. We need a call, even if it is only the call of the alarm clock. In this technological age we can even get our digital personal organiser to give us a call to remind us of our appointments. We are dealing with all kinds of calls throughout the day. The sound of the doorbell, the ringing of the phone, the dropping of a letter into our hall – are all calls of one kind or another. Some calls are more urgent than others. If the ringing of the phone is to tell us that a close relative or friend has suddenly taken seriously ill, we experience a strong call to respond immediately. Without having to think twice, we drop everything and set out on a journey. Because we value the person who has taken ill, everything else we might have been planning suddenly seems unimportant. A parent who hears a child crying in the middle of the night will respond immediately, no matter how tired he or she might be. Here is a call that simply cannot be ignored. All parents would be alike in that respect, because there is nothing they value more than the welfare of their child.

There is a close relationship between what we value and how we feel called. Fr Niall O'Brien was an Irish Columban priest who worked in the Philippines. Justice for the farmers who worked in the sugar plantations was a powerful value for him. Because such justice was being denied, he felt a strong call to work with the farmers for more just conditions. He could not but be faithful to that call, even when it meant being falsely accused and imprisoned. Many people have become involved in projects on behalf of children in Roumania and in Chernobyl. Because they hold the well-being of children as such a strong value, they experience a strong call to promote a fuller life for those children who have been traumatised by official neglect. Those values of truth, justice, reconciliation and fullness of life are gospel values. The call that they generate is a gospel call. The energy that drives people to pursue truth, justice, reconciliation and a fuller life for the most vulnerable is the energy of the Lord.

It is clear from the first reading this morning that a dominant value for Paul and Barnabas is what that reading calls 'the word of God', the good news that God had acted and was acting in the person of Jesus to bring salvation and fullness of life to men and women of every nation. Because Paul and Barnabas valued that good news so much, they experienced a strong call to preach the word of God to both Jews and Gentiles, even in the face of great hostility. In the second reading we are given an image of men and women of every nation who responded to that preached word. They so valued God's word, and the Lord who is at the centre of God's word, that they experienced a call to be faithful to the Lord even in spite of persecution. In the gospel reading, Jesus speaks of his disciples as those who listen to his voice, those who value his word and who, as a result, hear the call of that word and respond to it.

Today's readings invite us to reflect on the ways we feel called, on what it is we really value. We are invited today to renew our choice of the Lord as the dominant value of our lives. In the words of the Psalm we say: 'We are his people, the sheep of his flock.' If we value the Lord and all he stands for, we will listen to the voice of the good shepherd. As we grow in our relationship with the Lord, as we come to value him more deeply, we will hear his call more clearly. The call of the Lord will always be a call to value all that he values, such as the pursuit of truth, the work of justice, the task of reconciliation, the promotion of life in all its forms. The more we value the Lord and his gospel, the more sensitive we will be to the absence of truth, justice, reconciliation, and dignified living all around us, and the more we will feel called to address that absence.

Through our baptism, we have chosen the Lord and all he stands for as the dominant value of our lives. We pray that we would grow in our attentiveness to the voice of the Lord's call, and that we would never allow the Lord's voice to be drowned out by less significant voices.

Fifth Sunday of Easter

Most of us can think of people in our lives who encouraged us at a time when we needed encouragement. Such people probably encouraged us more by the quality of their presence to us than by anything they said. The way they were present with us helped us to find the energy to keep going. They may have helped us to see a value in what we were doing that we were slow to see for ourselves.

As in other areas of life, when it comes to our relationship with the Lord, and the living out of that relationship, we all need encouragement. St Paul in his letters was fond of calling on the members of his churches to encourage one another in their faith. When writing to the Thessalonians, for example, he says to them: 'Encourage one another and build up each other, as indeed you are doing.' In today's first reading we find Paul, along with Barnabas, engaged in that same ministry of encouragement. Luke tells us that Paul and Barnabas 'put fresh heart into the disciples, encouraging them to persevere in the faith'. In a sense, the primary role of a priest in a faith community is to be an encourager, to encourage people in their faith, in their relationship with the Lord. Nearly all priests would also say that they themselves receive great encouragement from the parish community in which they work. The struggle of people to persevere in the faith, even in the face of personal difficulty, is a great encouragement to priests. Paul's call to the church of Thessalonica to encourage one another and to build up each other reminds us that we are all called to be ministers of encouragement to each other. We all have a role to play in encouraging each other in the living of our baptismal faith.

That call to encourage one another is one expression of the Lord's call in the gospel reading to love one another as he has loved us. In the course of his public ministry, the Lord was very much engaged in the work of giving encouragement to people. One example of that is his first meeting with Peter. Peter said to Jesus, 'Depart from me for I am a sinful man,' and Jesus responded to him, 'Do not be afraid, from now on it is people you will catch.' That was at the very beginning of Jesus' ministry. Then at the very end of his ministry, after the last supper, he said to Peter, 'I have prayed for you, Simon, that your faith may not fail, and you, when once you have turned back, strengthen your brothers and sisters.' One of the ways the Lord encouraged others was by praying for them. One of the ways we encourage one another is by praying for each other. As a parish community, we are all called to pray for one another. We do that in a formal way in the prayers of intercession that conclude the liturgy of the word. The content of Jesus' prayer for Peter suggests one of the ways we might pray for each other. We pray for each other that our faith may not fail and that, when we do fail, we would always turn back, as Peter did, so that our failing and turning back would become an encouragement to others.

One of the important ways we encourage each other is by being people of hope, people who have a hopeful vision. The prophet called John who wrote the Book of Revelation was such a hopeful person. He was writing to churches that were struggling. He tried to encourage them by giving them a hopeful vision, a vision of the kingdom of God that God was working to bring about. One aspect of John's hopeful vision is given to us in this morning's second reading. He describes there a city which is penetrated with God's presence, where the inhabitants live as God's people, and from which death, mourning and sadness have been banished because God reigns. The city he describes is an image of the church at its best. It is also an image of what all our earthly cities are called to become. Here, indeed, is visionary and encouraging writing.

The church needs people of vision as much in the 21st century as it did in the 1st century. We need people to remind us of God's vision for our lives and for our world, and to keep us focused on that, lest we forget it. We all need to hold onto the vision of the kingdom that Jesus embodied by his life, death and resurrection, and to find ways of sharing it with each other. In this way we encourage each other and build each other up.

Sixth Sunday of Easter

We gather here for this Eucharist as people who have been baptised and confirmed. We associate the coming of the Holy Spirit with both of those moments in our lives. Yet, the action of the Holy Spirit in our lives is not confined to those two sacramental moments. The Holy Spirit engages with us and seeks to influence us throughout our lives. We need the Holy Spirit all through life. We are invited to pray the prayer, 'Come Holy Spirit', on a regular basis in the course of our journey through life.

In the gospel reading this morning, Jesus is taking his leave of his disciples at the last supper. He tries to reassure his troubled disciples that, although he will soon be taken from them, he will not be leaving them. He is going away, but he will return through the coming of the Holy Spirit. Jesus tells his disciples that, through that coming of the Spirit, both he and his Father will make their home with them. That wonderful promise that Jesus made to his disciples on the night before he died is also made to us. We are his disciples today. We may not always live as his disciples but, at least, we desire to love the Lord and to demonstrate our love by keeping his word. The Lord responds to that desire by giving us the same Holy Spirit that he promised to his disciples.

What do we look to the Holy Spirit for? In the gospel reading the Holy Spirit is called an Advocate, a kind of council for the defence. We look to the Holy Spirit to defend us against all that would damage our relationship with the Lord. We are aware that the culture in which we live is not always supportive of that relationship. There are many voices that take delight in trying to undermine our Christian faith. We look to the Holy Spirit to confirm us in our relationship with the Lord when that relationship comes under attack. Jesus was aware that his disciples would experience the same hostility that he experienced. That is one of the reasons why he promised to send them an Advocate who would stand alongside them to strengthen them when their faith was put to the test.

What else do we look to the Holy Spirit for? In the gospel reading, Jesus tells his disciples that the Holy Spirit will teach them everything and remind them of all that he has said to them. Those words of Jesus suggest that his disciples must always remain learners. When it comes to our relationship with the Lord we are always learners. We have to keep relearning what it means to be a follower of Jesus in today's world. We need the Holy Spirit to teach us what it means to live the gospel in the concrete circumstances of our own lives. The Spirit reminds us of all that Jesus said to us, not just in some general way, but as it relates to the unique circumstances of our lives. We need the light of the Holy Spirit every day. In today's second reading, we are told that the heavenly city did not need the sun or the moon for light, since it was lit by the radiant glory of God. Something of that heavenly light comes to us in this life through the Holy Spirit.

What else might we look to the Holy Spirit for? The first reading this morning suggests that the Holy Spirit has a special role to play in resolving conflict. That reading describes a significant moment of conflict in the life of the early church. Should converts to Christ from paganism be asked to keep the Jewish law? There were two views on this, both of them passionately argued for. In this moment of conflict, the church sought the guidance of the Holy Spirit. The final decision was reached with the help of the Holy Spirit. We are no strangers to conflict ourselves, whether it is in our church, our families or the wider world. We need the help of the Holy Spirit if we are to resolve our conflicts well. In the gospel reading, Jesus speaks of the gift of his own peace, a peace the world cannot give. Such peace is the fruit of the Holy Spirit. We need to pray, 'Come Holy Spirit', and to be open to the influence of the Spirit if our conflicts are to be resolved in ways that lead to lasting peace and reconciliation. We will be celebrating the feast of Pentecost in two weeks time. The readings this morning prompt us to look forward to that feast, and to prepare for it by praying for a new outpouring of the Holy Spirit into our lives.

Feast of the Ascension

We live in a fast-moving age. It is very noticeable if you drive a car. You can be driving along at what you consider to be a reasonable speed, and you become conscious of a car bearing down on you, waiting for the first available opportunity to pass you out. In such a situation you can feel under pressure to go faster. Everyone seems to be in a hurry. In that context, waiting can go against the grain. We often experience waiting as something negative. If we have to wait longer than we were expecting to wait, we can get very impatient.

Yet, we know from experience that waiting is a necessary part of life. There are certain things that cannot be rushed. If we become ill, we know we have to wait until we recover sufficiently before taking up our normal pace again. That is equally true when it comes to how we relate to others. A new born child will grow at a certain rate. Parents adjust themselves to the child's pace. They would never try to force a child to walk before he or she is ready. In our dealing with other adults, we often have to learn to wait as well. Everyone has their own pace and rhythm. We might come to clarity about something very quickly, whereas it might take others longer to come to the same clarity. The temptation not to wait but to go ahead on our own can be strong. Yet, waiting is not only respectful of the other person, it can also serve us well. By having to wait we can learn something that we might not otherwise have learnt.

Today we celebrate the feast of the Ascension. A moment came when Jesus was no longer present to his disciples in a visible, bodily form. Before taking his leave of them, he commissioned them to preach the gospel to all nations, beginning from Jerusalem. However, before the disciples were to set out on that mission, Jesus called on them to wait. He said to them, in the words of the first reading, 'Wait in Jerusalem for what the Father had promised.' The temptation for the disciples might have been to get straight down to work. The Lord's work is urgent; there is no time to waste. Yet, the Lord asked them to take their time, to wait. In a sense, he was asking them to work according to the Lord's time, rather than their own time. After all, it was the Lord's work they were being asked to do, not their own work. The time of waiting was an opportunity to adjust themselves to the Lord's rhythm, rather than their own. In calling on them to wait until they were clothed with power from on high, Jesus was reminding them that the Lord of the work was more important than the work of the Lord, and that they could really only do the work of the Lord in the strength that the Lord provided.

The feast of the Ascension reminds us that, as well as learning to wait on ourselves and on each other, we also need to wait on the Lord. The Lord says to all of us what he says to his first disciples in that first reading: 'You shall be my witnesses.' He asks all of us to be his visible, bodily expression in the world. If we are to be faithful to that calling, we need to learn to wait on the Lord. The primary way we wait on the Lord is through prayer. That is how the first disciples understood the Lord's call to wait. The end of the gospel reading tells us that after the Lord ascended they went back to Jerusalem, where they were continually in the Temple praising God.

For us too, waiting on the Lord takes the form of prayer. In prayer we open ourselves to receive from the Lord all that we need in order to be his witnesses in the world. That is why prayer is at the heart of our lives as Christians, whether it is the public prayer of the church, such as the Eucharist, or our own personal prayer. We often think of prayer as asking God for something. More fundamentally, prayer is about waiting. Prayer is more about waiting on what the Lord wants to give us than about asking him for what we want. Such prayer of waiting does not always need words. It is an attitude of heart, and silence can express that attitude of heart more fully than any words we might speak. The feast of the Ascension invites us to enter more fully into that prayer of waiting as we prepare ourselves for the feast of Pentecost next Sunday.

Seventh Sunday of Easter

Most of us will have been taught certain prayers at school. As children we may have learnt these prayers by heart. We were then able to recite them as the occasion arose. As we grew older we may have found that the prayers we learnt by heart as children were not enough for us. Although we continued to pray them, we also found that we needed to speak to God in our own words, as well as in words that were given to us. We wanted to communicate with God personally about the things that were important to us, and the people who were significant for us. As adults we may have found that our way of praying has changed over the years. We may discover, for example, that silence can come to play a bigger role in our prayer. You may have heard the story of the elderly man who used to come into a particular church every morning for an hour. Someone asked him once what he did during the hour and he simply replied, 'He looks at me and I look at him.'

One form of prayer that comes easy to many of us is the prayer of intercession. If we are close to someone, and if we are people of prayer at all, we will invariably find ourselves praying for that person. We carry those we love and care about in our hearts and minds, and if prayer is the lifting up of the heart and mind to God, as an older catechism expressed it, we will from time to time lift up those who are in our hearts and minds to God. Our prayer for them is an expression of our love for them. In bringing them before the Lord we believe that we are in some way opening them up to the Lord's life-giving presence. Who we pray for, and how we pray for them, can say a lot about who we are and how we relate.

There are two examples of this prayer of intercession in today's readings. In the first reading, Stephen, who was the first Christian martyr, prays for his executioners, 'Lord, do not hold this sin against them.' The focus of most of our prayers of intercession is our loved ones. The focus of Stephen's prayer of intercession was his enemies. Here indeed is an extraordinarily generous prayer of intercession. It corresponds to how Jesus asked us to pray: 'Bless those who curse you, pray for those who abuse you' (Lk 6:28). It is how Jesus prayed himself, according to Luke, as he hung from the cross: 'Father, forgive them; for they do not know what they are doing' (Lk 23:34). Stephen's prayer was very much in the spirit of Jesus' own prayer. The Holy Spirit is the source of all authentic prayer. As the Holy Spirit is the Spirit of Jesus, we can expect that the Holy Spirit will move us from time to time to pray for those who have shown themselves hostile to us. How often do we pray for those who have hurt us? – Perhaps, not very often. It is not an easy prayer to make. Yet, it is perhaps how Jesus would want to pray within us. If we cannot bring ourselves to pray such a prayer, we might be able to express to the Lord our desire to pray such a prayer and to ask his help in making it.

The second example of the prayer of intercession in today's readings is Jesus' own prayer of intercession in the gospel reading. Here Jesus is not praying for his enemies but for those whom he has declared to be his friends. He prays for his disciples who are present to him on the night before he dies, and for future generations of disciples, for you and me gathered here today. His prayer for us expresses his desire for us. There are two parts to his prayer for us in today's gospel reading. He prays that his disciples may be completely one as he and his Father are one, and he also prays that beyond this life his disciples would be where he now is, in his Father's house where there are many dwelling places (Jn 14:2). His prayer relates to our present and to our future. His vision for our lives now and his vision for our lives beyond this life are intimately related. If our final destiny is to be with him, our present calling is to allow him to be with us and among us, or in the words of the gospel reading, to allow his love to be in us and among us. We are made for communion, communion with each other in the Lord both in this life and in the next.

Feast of Pentecost

When it gets very warm, people like to head to the seaside. The cooling breeze at the coast can be very refreshing on a warm day. We know that wind can be very damaging, but it can also be very invigorating and life-giving.

That is how St Luke wants us to understanding his reference to wind in his description of the first Pentecost in today's first reading. He was saying that the coming of the Holy Spirit on the first disciples was like a life-giving and invigorating wind. It renewed and refreshed their desire to become the Lord's witnesses in the world and to share in the Lord's work. The first disciples needed Pentecost after the rigours of Jesus' passion and death. Their faith had been put in crisis by the crucifixion of Jesus. Pentecost transformed them. The coming of the Holy Spirit filled them with new energy and enthusiasm for the Lord. According to the first reading, they began preaching the gospel boldly in a way that everyone could understand.

Most of us, at some time in our lives, will have had a similar experience to those first disciples. For one reason or another, our faith can grown weak. We can lose sight of the Lord; the enthusiasm we once had for the gospel can diminish. This loss of enthusiasm can happen very quickly, perhaps because of some Good Friday experience in our lives, some devastating loss in which we felt abandoned by the Lord. Or it can creep up on us over time in a very gradual way. There can be many reasons for that happening. The parable of the sower makes reference to the cares of the world, the lure of wealth, the desire for other things. To that list we might add the human frailty of church leaders, the frustration with what we experience as unanswered prayer, the lack of supports for our own faith life in a culture that is becoming increasingly secular. For a whole variety of reasons, our faith can grow weak over time, and our relationship with the Lord can become less significant for us. It is then above all that we need the Holy Spirit to blow afresh on us and to breathe new life into the dry bones of our relationship with the Lord. The Holy Spirit refreshes and renews our faith, hope and love. We need the constant coming of the Holy Spirit to enliven us, to keep us fresh as followers of Jesus, to fan the embers of our faith into a living flame. Even if we do not explicitly ask the Holy Spirit to blow afresh on us, the Spirit works in our lives anyway.

St Paul was very clear that the Holy Spirit is always at work in the lives of those who have been baptised, even when we are not conscious of the Spirit's presence. He tells the baptised Christians in Rome in today's second reading: 'The Spirit of God has made his home in you ... the Spirit of him who raised Jesus from the dead is living in you.' The same words are addressed to us this morning. The Holy Spirit has made his home in us in virtue of our baptism. Paul tells us that the Spirit we have received has made us sons and daughters of God, sharers in Christ's own relationship with God. As a result, the Spirit is always prompting us to cry out 'Abba, Father' to God, as Jesus did. The Spirit we received in baptism is always at work in our lives, assuring us that we are God's beloved sons and daughters, prompting us to relate to God as Jesus does.

That work of the Spirit in our lives never ceases. The Spirit within us cries out to God, 'Abba, Father', even when we do not join in that prayer. In other words, even when we give up praying, the Spirit within us does not cease to pray. Even when we have ceased to relate to God in any conscious way, the Spirit within us continues to relate to God on our behalf. There is always much more going on between ourselves and God than we realise, even during those times when the flame of faith appears to be very weak. In the words of the gospel reading this morning, the Holy Spirit never ceases to remind us of what Jesus has said to us. The Holy Spirit remains our teacher even when we are not disposed to learning. The Spirit will not let us forget. This is another way of saying that the Lord remains faithful to us, even when we have grown faithless. The feast of Pentecost is an opportunity to renew our own fidelity by welcoming the work of the Spirit in our lives.

Feast of the Most Holy Trinity

The French philosopher, Jean Paul Sartre, once wrote, 'Hell is other people.' There are times in our lives when we might find it easy to sympathise with that sentiment. If we have had a very negative experience of other people over a period of time, we can long to be on our own, away from the troubles that others seem to bring us. We can begin to think of heaven as a state of glorious isolation. Yet, even the greatest loners among us long for human company and companionship from time to time. At some deep level we sense that we are only complete when we are in relationship with others. Solitary confinement is a very cruel form of punishment for a prisoner. It is the frustration of a very deep need in all of us to be present to others and to have others present to us. We all long for some form of communion with others. If we were to call to mind the happiest moments of our lives, we would probably discover that they involved some element of communion, some experience of relationship. Even in our age of great individualism, we know instinctively that no one is an island.

Today's feast of the Trinity reminds us that what is true of ourselves is even truer of God. At the very heart of God's own life is a communion of persons who relate in perfect harmony. Within God there is a relationship of profound love between the Father, the Son, and the Holy Spirit. That community of love within God is not closed in on itself but is open to all of us. The love between the Father, Son and Holy Spirit reaches out to embrace us all. As Paul says in today's second reading, 'The love of God has been poured into our hearts by the Holy Spirit that has been given to us.' Through the Holy Spirit, we are continually drawn into the life of the Trinity. According to this morning's gospel reading, the Holy Spirit reminds us of what Jesus said to us, taking from the words of Jesus and telling them to us. The work of the Holy Spirit is to lead us to the Son, enabling us to have the same relationship with God that Jesus has, prompting us to cry out 'Abba, Father' as Jesus does. We come to God the Father, through the Son, in the Spirit.

As people who share in the life of the Trinity, we have a mission from God to create communities of love, communities that somehow reflect the community of the Trinity. The first community of love that we experience is our family. We are born into a family. None of us have perfect families. We will always struggle with our families in one way or another. Yet, within our family we are called to play our part in forming a community of love that reflects and gives expression to that love that is within God. Beyond the family, the church is called to be a community of love. Jesus, on the night before he died, said to his disciples, 'As the Father has loved me, I have loved you … Love one another as I have loved you.' Jesus wants the church to be a loving community that is a reflection of the loving community that is God. We know that the church, the gathering of Jesus' disciples, has frequently fallen short of this vision of Jesus. Yet, the Holy Spirit keeps on reminding us of what we are called to be as church. The parish is the local church, and every parish is called to be a reflection of the loving communion that is God. With the Spirit's help we are called to make of our parish a community of love. The parish has been well described as a community of communities.

If we look around us we will find examples of communities of love that are not specifically church related. There is a whole range of support groups for various categories of people. Many adults put energy and time into bringing children together in ways that are life-giving and formative. Whenever we work to make such communities possible we are acting in a Trinitarian way, even if we have no awareness of the Trinity when we are doing it. Every time we bring people together in ways that affirm them and build them up, we are living in the spirit of the Trinity. That is the call and the challenge of today's feast. Although the feast of the Trinity might initially seem remote from us, it is, in reality, a very down to earth feast, because it reminds us of what we need to be about in our day-to-day lives.

Feast of Corpus Christi

The Latin name 'Corpus Christi' may not be easily understood by many people today. The title, 'The Body and Blood of Christ' is probably more intelligible. Today is the feast of the Eucharist, a day when we give thanks for the gift of the Eucharist, through which the Lord is present among us in a very special way.

In the opening pages of his encyclical on the Eucharist, the late Pope John Paul II recalled the many places in which he celebrated the Eucharist. He mentions that he celebrated Mass in the great basilicas and churches in Rome and throughout the world, in chapels built along mountain paths, on lakeshores and sea-coasts, on altars built in stadiums and in city squares. He remarks that the great variety of places where he has celebrated Mass has given him a powerful experience of the universal and cosmic character of the Eucharist. As he puts it, 'Even when the Eucharist is celebrated on the humble altar of a country church, it is always in some way celebrated on the altar of the world.' The Eucharist, he says, 'embraces and permeates all creation'.

In John's gospel, Jesus, speaking of his death, says: 'When I am lifted up from the earth, I will draw all people to myself.' He gave his life in love so as to draw all people to himself and to the God who sent him. It is that self-giving love of Jesus unto death that we celebrate in the Eucharist and that is present to us there. Christ present in the Eucharist continues to draw all people, all of creation, to himself. That is why, whenever we gather to celebrate the Eucharist, we are invited to think globally, to remember all of humanity, all of creation.

The Eucharist will always invite us to broaden our horizons, to look beyond ourselves, beyond our families, our parish, our diocese, towards all of humanity and all of creation. The Eucharist puts it up to us to have the same breadth of vision that Jesus had. Something of Jesus' breadth of vision is reflected in today's gospel reading. The crowds to whom Jesus had been ministering had grown hungry. The disciples suggested that Jesus send the crowds away. Their suggestion revealed a certain narrowness of vision on their part. They wanted the problem crowd removed from the scene. However, Jesus' horizon was wider than that of his disciples. He challenged his disciples to engage with the crowd. 'Give them something to eat your-selves,' he said to them. The disciples resisted Jesus' suggestion, claiming that the task was beyond them, 'We have no more than five loaves and two fish.' Jesus went on to show them that he could work powerfully with their limited resources and that, with his help, the task they had considered impossible was in-deed manageable. Jesus enabled his disciples to feed the very crowd they had been so keen to dismiss.

We might be able to recognise something of ourselves in the disciples. We too can allow our horizon to become narrowed to what we consider to be manageable. The Lord in the Eucharist will always prompt us to look beyond our own narrow circle and to enter more fully into his own generous vision. In the sec-ond reading this morning, Paul tells us that Jesus instituted the Eucharist 'on the night he was betrayed'. Those words of Paul bring us back to the dramatic setting in which the Eucharist was born. The Eucharist is intimately linked to the events of the Lord's passion and death. The Lord's death on the cross was a death for all, an expression of a love that knows no measure.

Whenever we celebrate the Eucharist, we are expressing our desire that something of this universal scope of the Lord's love we are celebrating would be present in our own lives. To cele-brate the Eucharist is to commit ourselves to the same generous vision that characterised Jesus' life and death, the vision whose instinct it is to feed the hungry crowd rather than send them away. The invitation we are given at Mass to offer each other the sign of peace is a small reminder of the call that the Eucharist makes on us to move beyond our own narrow circle. As Christ challenged his disciples in today's gospel reading, the Eucharist challenges us to engage with people we might initially be tempted to send away. Today on the feast of Corpus Christi we give thanks for the many people in our parish and beyond who live the Eucharist they celebrate, who make present in their own lives something of the universal charity of Christ. We pray that our own vision would be stretched by the universal sacrifice of the Eucharist that we celebrate every Sunday.

Second Sunday in Ordinary Time

I remember as a child growing up that whenever somebody ran out of some commodity, they could go to a neighbour and get what they needed. One week you might be the person in need. The next week you might be the one who gave to the neighbour in need. To a great extent, that particular expression of neighbourliness belongs to an era that is past. It reflects a time when people did not have fridges or freezers. Today, we are more self-reliant, and we would probably find it much more difficult to go asking from neighbours in that way.

The gospel reading of the wedding guests running out of wine brought to my mind that distant memory of people running out of things unexpectedly. Wine was the primary drink for people in Jesus' time and place. To run out of wine, especially on an occasion like a wedding, would be like running out of some very basic drink, like water, today. As individuals or as families, we may not run out of food or drink very often, but we can run out in other ways. We can make too many demands on ourselves over a long period of time, and one day we discover that we have run out of energy; the tank is empty. The wine runs out, as it were. Or some great disappointment can drain away our enthusiasm for life. We might have put a lot of ourselves into something and have met with rejection or failure. As a result, our sense of initiative or adventure runs out on us, and we decide to play it safe from then on. When we lose someone significant through death or through separation of some other kind, our hope and our joy can run out on us. We find ourselves in a despondent and joyless place. The future seems very bleak without this person to share it with. At such times, we can easily identify with the two names given to Israel in the first reading, 'Forsaken', 'Abandoned'. A whole family can also run out of some basic quality. Some row or dispute brings new levels of tension and disharmony into the family. The cohesion that was once there runs out. There is a real sense of loss, of something important having run out.

In a whole variety of ways, the wine can run out on us. Today's readings are a word of encouragement to us when we find ourselves in that kind of situation of loss. At Cana, the Lord worked not just to replace what had run out but to surpass what had run out. He not only replaced the wine but he provided wine of a better quality. As the steward of the feast said to the bridegroom, 'You have kept the best wine till now.' The Lord did not do this by himself. It required the involvement of others. It was his mother who first brought the problem to the Lord's attention and then gave instructions to the servants. The servants in turn did everything that Jesus asked them to do. The Lord worked through those present to bring new life out of a situation of great loss.

The same Lord continues to work in the same way today, working creatively in our situations of loss. He continues to serve those for whom the wine has run out but, as in the gospel reading, he needs people through whom he can work. In the second reading, Paul speaks of God working in all sorts of different ways in different people, and refers to the Holy Spirit who distributes different gifts to different people for the good of others. The Lord, through the Spirit, has gifted all of us in ways that enable us to support those struggling with loss.

Our role in helping to change a situation of loss into one of abundance might be a very simple one, as simple as Mary's role at Cana. Her role was one of intercession. She brought the situation of loss to the Lord's attention. The Spirit that we have received at baptism often inspires us to play that role of intercessor. One of the ways we serve each other is by praying for each other, interceding with the Lord on each other's behalf. We bring before the Lord in prayer those for whom the wine has run out. At Cana, Mary's work of intercession was complemented by the physical work of the servants who filled the jars with water. The Spirit sometimes moves us to do something very practical for those who feel drained and empty. We pray that we would always be open to the many ways the Lord wants to work through us to serve those for whom something basic has run out.

Third Sunday in Ordinary Time

When we hear the term 'Body of Christ' we probably instinctively think of the Eucharist, the body of Christ that we receive in the Eucharist. The term 'Body of Christ' also refers, of course, to all of us who gather to celebrate the Eucharist, the community of the baptised.

That is how Paul uses the term in the second reading this morning. He tells the Corinthians, 'You are the body of Christ.' If Paul were standing here this morning, he would address the same words to all of us. Paul does not say to the Corinthians or to us, 'If you do this, or if you live in this way, then you will become the body of Christ.' He says, 'You are the body of Christ.' In a similar way, we who gather here this morning do not have to become the body of Christ. All of us are already members of Christ's body. As Paul says in our reading, we were baptised in the one Spirit, and that baptism in the Spirit has made us members of Christ's body. This was a gift that was given to us at a very early age. We did not have to earn it. Before we were capable of deserving anything, we were graced by God in this extraordinary way – baptised into Christ, made members of Christ's body. For that, we give thanks to God every day.

Paul in that reading compares the body of Christ, the church, to a human body. Just as a human body has great diversity, he says, so also has the body of Christ. There is tremendous diversity within the church, within the local church here in this parish. Although the one Spirit has made us all members of one body, that Spirit has graced us all in different ways. As members of Christ's body we each show a different aspect of the richness of Christ. If Christ is to express his richness through us, the members of his body, he needs to express himself in different ways through different people. No one of us, no matter how gifted we are, can do justice to the richness of Christ. The Spirit enables each of us to reveal Christ in our own unique way, in a way that corresponds to our natural abilities and temperament. If there is too much uniformity in the body of Christ, then Christ will not be able to express himself fully in the world. Paul says in the second reading: 'If your whole body was just one eye, how would you hear anything? If it was just one ear, how could it smell anything?' The Spirit is always at work creating diversity in the one body of Christ because, without that diversity, we the church would not be able to reveal Christ properly.

The particular way that the Spirit has graced each one of us is vital for the full functioning of Christ's body. For that reason, we each need to value our place in the church, and to appreciate the unique role that only I can play. None of us in the church can ever say, paraphrasing today's second reading, 'Because I am not this that or the other I do not belong to the body.' In stating, 'I do not belong', we sell ourselves short, and we sell everybody else in the church short as well, because we are dependant on each other. If my gifts are needed by others, it is equally true that I stand in need of those who have been gifted in different ways to me. That is why, as Paul says in the second reading, 'The eye cannot say to the hand, "I do not need you".' We can sometimes send out that signal to others in the body of Christ, without always being aware of it.

It is only when all the members of Christ's body are making the contribution that the Spirit enables them to make, that, in the words of the gospel reading, the poor will hear good news, captives will be freed, and the blind will receive new sight. The programme that Jesus outlined for himself in his inaugural sermon in Nazareth was not only a programme for his own ministry. It is also a programme for his body the church. The Spirit has gifted all of us in different ways to enable us as Christ's body to continue Christ's work, as he outlined it in Nazareth. It is the church's calling to proclaim the year of the Lord's favour, especially to those who are struggling. We pray this morning that each of us would be open to the particular way the Spirit is gifting us, so that the Lord's life-giving work, begun in Nazareth, might continue through us today.

Fourth Sunday in Ordinary Time

We all have to come to terms with people disagreeing with us and rejecting our ideas and proposals. There is no avoiding the cut and thrust that is inevitable in our day-to-day dealings with people. However, to experience rejection of myself as a person takes a great deal more out of me. The most extreme form of rejecting others is to kill them. Personal rejection can take much less extreme forms. The break up of relationships and friendships can be accompanied by a sense of personal rejection on the part of one or both of the parties involved. The wounds inflicted by such an experience of personal rejection will often be healed only by the opposite experience over time of a love that is faithful and enduring.

What makes rejection all the more difficult to bear is when we are rejected by someone who initially accepted and loved us. The resulting feeling of personal diminishment can take a long time to work through. The gospel reading today shows Jesus being rejected by those who initially accepted him. When he went to his home town of Nazareth and preached there, initially 'he won the approval of all'; people 'were astonished by the gracious words that came from his lips'. Within a relatively short space of time, that acceptance changed to scepticism, 'This is Joseph's son, surely?' and, finally, to outright and murderous rejection: 'They took him up to the brow of the hill their town was built on, intending to throw him down the cliff.'

Sometimes we have little control over the drift from initial acceptance to rejection by someone or some group. We might be able to forestall this shift by surrendering our deepest convictions so as to comply with the expectations of others. Jesus would not have been rejected by the people of Nazareth if he had become the kind of parochial figure they wanted him to be, instead of declaring himself to be a prophet whose mission was not only to the people of Israel but also to the pagan peoples beyond Israel. Yet, Jesus knew that he had to be true to his God-given mission. Acceptance by others is not of such a value that it needs to be bought at the price of denying our deepest convictions. Integrity – remaining true to God's promptings – is a much higher value than finding acceptance. A certain amount of rejection may be the price we have to pay if we are to take the path we know in good conscience we must take. Giving in to what other people want to order to keep them on our side can lead to some short term gain, but in the end it can be more damaging to ourselves than the rejection we avoided by our compliance.

Although we may have little control over the drift from initial acceptance to rejection, we do have some control over how we deal with the experience of rejection. We can allow that experience to make us bitter and resentful. This is not how Jesus dealt with his experience of rejection. The gospel reading tells us that, in response to his rejection in Nazareth, he 'slipped through the crowd and walked away'. Jesus continued on with his mission of proclaiming the good news of God's favour to all people, including those who had rejected him. Likewise, when he experienced a much more painful rejection in Jerusalem, Luke tells us that he prayed, 'Father, forgive them for they know not what they do.' Jesus was not embittered by rejection because he was rooted and grounded in God's love.

Paul's description of love in the second reading is, in reality, a portrait of the God in whom Jesus was grounded and whom he reveals. This is a God who is always patient and kind, who takes no pleasure in other people's sins, who is always ready to excuse, to trust, to hope, whose love does not come to an end. Such a love is capable of holding us together when the experience of rejection threatens to break us apart. Such a love can prevent us from drifting into bitterness and resentment. Paul was very aware that everything passes, even the wonderful gifts of the Holy Spirit. What does not pass, he says, is God's love for us in Christ. In this life we may only see a dim reflection of this love. In eternity we will experience this love to the full, as we see God face to face. The faith conviction that God's love for us does not come to an end keeps us strong, even when we struggle with the agonising experience of rejection. That same faith conviction empowers us to reveal something of that same love to others who have experienced rejection.

Fifth Sunday in Ordinary Time

In the course of a week we normally find ourselves in a whole variety of places. We will spend a certain amount of time in our home and, very likely, some of us will spend much more time in our place of work. We will spend some time in places where we can relax, and some people, like yourselves here this morning, will spend time in the parish church on a Sunday or perhaps at other times of the week as well. We might be inclined to think that our time in church is 'religious' time, and our time everywhere else is 'secular' time. We can presume that it is primarily in the sacred space of the church that the Lord relates to us and we relate to him.

The readings this morning invite us to have a broader view of what constitutes religious time and sacred space. In the first reading and the gospel reading, two people have a profound experience of the Lord, a man of Jerusalem named Isaiah and a man of Galilee named Simon. Isaiah encountered the Lord's powerful presence in what Jews would have considered to be the most sacred space on earth, the sanctuary of the temple in Jerusalem. His overwhelming experience of the Lord's holiness in that sacred place made him more sensitive to his own sinfulness and that of his people: 'I am a man of unclean lips and I live among a people of unclean lips.' Simon had an equally powerful experience of the Lord's presence, not while at prayer in the temple of Jerusalem, but while he was engaged in his daily work as a fisherman by the Sea of Galilee. His reaction to that experience of the Lord's presence was very similar to Isaiah's: 'I am a sinful man.'

The gospel reading this morning invites us to be sensitive to the Lord's presence and call in all the many places where we find ourselves in the course of our week. The Lord does not confine himself to our churches, and we need not restrict our relationship to him to the times when we are in church. The risen Lord comes to us under many guises. Simon's more ordinary experience of the Lord as he went about his daily chores will be more the norm for most of us than Isaiah's more extraordinary one. In the gospels the very ordinary way in which the risen Lord came to his disciples often resulted in their not recognising him initially. The two disciples on the road to Emmaus thought he was just another visitor to Jerusalem, and Mary Magdalene thought he was the gardener. The Lord comes to us in and through the ordinary people and circumstances of our lives, and it is there that we hear his call. Furthermore, the experience of his presence and his call are not the prerogative of those who are a long way down the road of spiritual maturity. Both Isaiah and Simon were very aware that they were far from being all they could be. Paul in today's second reading was equally clear about that fact; he continues to be amazed that the risen Lord appeared to him even though he persecuted the church of God. The Lord, it seems, is not fussy about the company he keeps, and he calls very imperfect people into his service. He is present to you and to me, and he is calling you and me, in all our imperfection.

The Lord's call will take different forms for each one of us, but it will always be, in some shape or form, a call to 'put out into deep water', in the words of today's gospel reading. The Lord calls us to deepen our relationship with him, to grow in our understanding of and in our living of the faith. He will also very often call us to take some initiative to help others in deepening their own relationship with the Lord. When the Lord calls us he always does so for the sake of others; his calling is at the same time a sending. Isaiah was sent to the people of Jerusalem, Simon was sent to his fellow Jews and Paul was sent to the Gentiles. For most of us, the people for whose sake we are called and to whom we are sent will be those among whom we live and work, with whom we have daily contact. Our initial response to our sense of the Lord's presence and call may be that of Simon, 'Leave me, Lord; I am a sinful man.' We may find it difficult to take ourselves as seriously as the Lord does. Hopefully, however, our final response will be that of Isaiah: 'Here I am, send me.'

Sixth Sunday in Ordinary Time

I was fortunate enough to visit the Holy Land the year before the present conflict began. I remember being in a part of the land that was quite barren and noticing the impact that the river Jordan made on that barren land. On either side of the river was a green line of vegetation that from a distance looked like a large green snake making its way through the barren landscape. It brought home to me the life-giving power of flowing water, even in an arid landscape. Today's first reading and responsorial psalm put me in mind of that scene. Jeremiah refers to a 'tree by the waterside that thrusts its roots to the stream', whose 'foliage stays green' and that 'never ceases to bear fruit'. The responsorial psalm makes reference to a 'tree that is planted beside the flowing waters, that yields its fruit in due season and whose leaves shall never fade'. For both Jeremiah and the psalmist the tree by the water that never ceases to bear fruit and that remains green, even in time of drought, is an image of those who have placed their trust in the Lord, and whose lives are rooted in the Lord.

Any one of us can find ourselves in a period of drought at some point in our lives, when life seems barren and harsh. It is a struggle to keep going; the elements seem to be against us. What keeps us going when we find ourselves in those inhospitable places? What prevents us from drying up and shrinking into ourselves, when we experience life as something of a wilderness? The first reading and the psalm suggest that it is our connection with the Lord that keeps us vibrant and fruitful, even when the place in which we find ourselves threatens to drain us of life. We do not have to bring about that connection with the Lord ourselves. The Lord, through his life, death and resurrection, and the sending of the Spirit, has drawn us to himself. We have only to respond to that initiative of the Lord. Our presence here this morning at this Eucharist is a sign that we have responded. Our calling is to keep on responding to the initiative that the Lord keeps taking towards us in drawing us to himself.

When Jesus looked out on his disciples in this morning's gospel reading, he recognised people who were in something of a wilderness. He addresses his disciples as poor, hungry and weeping. Life had become more of a struggle for them since they left their nets to follow him. Getting involved in Jesus' way of doing things had brought new demands, and had left them poorer, more vulnerable. Yet, Jesus declares to his struggling disciples that they are blessed because, in responding to his call, they would come to experience the abundance of God's generosity.

Our own efforts to respond to the Lord's initiative will make demands on us too; it will often mean taking the path less travelled. Some people looking at our lives might see us as losing out. Yet, the Lord assures us that what we might put aside in order to be faithful to him will seem very little in comparison to what we will receive from him. We will find true happiness in responding to the Lord's call. Our lives will be like a tree planted by flowing waters.

In the gospel reading, the Lord makes a promise to his struggling disciples: 'Yours is the kingdom of God.' The same promise is made to disciples in every generation. That promise begins to be fulfilled for us in this life. We begin to experience the presence of the kingdom of God, as we come to know the Lord's strength in our weakness, the Lord's life in our barren times. We believe, however, that we will only experience the fullness of God's kingdom in the next life. Paul says in the second reading, 'If our hope in Christ has been for this life only, we are the most unfortunate of all people.' We look forward in hope to that eternal moment when, in the words of the book of Revelation, the Lamb will guide his followers to springs of the water of life.

The gospel reading suggests that appearances can be deceptive. Those who seem to be loosing out, because they place their trust in the Lord rather than in themselves are, in reality, blessed. Those who seem to have it all are in reality unfortunate, in so far as their trust is only in themselves. The readings today invite us to root our lives in the Lord, and to go where he takes us, in the conviction that he is leading us to springs of living water.

Seventh Sunday in Ordinary Time

It can be important for an organisation to have a spokesperson, someone who can speak on behalf of everyone else. If an organisation appears to have several spokespersons, each saying something different, the result is confusion. No one knows where the organisation really stands. When it is a matter of individuals, rather than of organisations, we might be inclined to think that the problem of more than one spokesperson does not arise. Each individual is his or her own spokesperson. One person only has one voice. Yet, perhaps the situation is not as simple as that. If we are honest with ourselves we will probably recognise that, as individuals, we often speak with more than one voice. We can say one thing to one person and say something quite contrary to another. We do not always speak with one voice; we are not always consistent.

Perhaps one of the reasons we do not always speak with one voice is that we hear different voices within ourselves. We often find ourselves pulled in two different directions at once. We hear the voice of the Lord, the voice of conscience if you like, and, at the same time, we can hear another voice which is not of the Lord. At times we respond to the Lord's voice, and give expression to it in what we say and do; at other times we might give expression to that other voice. Because we do not consistently listen to the Lord's voice, we often end up speaking with different voices, sometimes in a way that is of the Lord and, at other times, in a way that is not.

A version of those two contrary voices that we sometimes hear within ourselves is to be found in today's first reading. When David and his commander Abishai came upon their enemy Saul, they reacted to his presence in two very different ways; they spoke with very different voices. Abishai spoke as one who wanted to pin Saul to the ground with Saul's own spear. David reacted in a very different way; he spoke with a very different voice. Addressing Abishai he said, 'Do not kill him, for who can lift his hand against the Lord's anointed?' It could be said that Abishai's voice was the more expected voice; he reacted in the way that any soldier would react when he came upon his enemy in a vulnerable position. Abishai's voice was

80

the voice of what Paul calls in the second reading, 'the first man, Adam', the man 'from the earth'. David's voice, in contrast, from a merely human point of view, was the more exceptional voice. It could be said that his was the voice of what Paul calls in that reading, 'the last Adam', 'the heavenly man', who is Christ.

In a sense, each one of us has something of both David and Abishai, something of the first Adam and of the last Adam, within us. When faced with a situation similar to the one that faced David and Abishai we can react in a manner that reflects the way of Adam who rebelled against God or in a manner that reflects the way of Christ who was faithful to God unto death. We can act out of sin or out of grace. Although there are those two possibilities, we believe that the power of grace is stronger in our lives than the power of sin. As Paul says in his letter to the Romans: 'Where sin abounds, grace abounds all the more.' Through faith and baptism we are of the heavenly man much more than we are of the earthly man. We live in Christ and Christ lives in us. Christ is always at work in our lives, living out his life in us.

When we hear today's gospel reading, we might be tempted to dismiss it as unliveable. How can we possibly love our enemy or do good to those who treat us badly? How can we be compassionate as God is compassionate? Yet, Jesus preached the message of today's gospel because he believed it could be lived. He did not present it as a piece of moral teaching to be admired but as a way of life to be lived. We cannot live this way of life by ourselves. Only Christ can live this life in us. Our calling is to keep on growing in our relationship with Christ, allowing him to grow in us, so that he can live this life in and through us. When that happens, his voice will come to dominate our lives, and we will begin to speak with one voice, the voice of Christ. We will begin to take one path, the path of Christ, regardless of how people might be treating us.

Eighth Sunday in Ordinary Time

We relish the experience of our national football team or our native county team winning an important match. Victory is sweet, as they say. For every victory, of course, there is also a defeat. While some rejoice, others grieve. Occasionally you hear people talk of a win-win situation, where there are only victors and no losers. Everyone gains in this situation.

This is the kind of victory that Paul speaks about today in the second reading when he exhorts: 'Let us thank God for giving us the victory through our Lord Jesus Christ.' The victory that Christ has given us is the victory over death: 'Death is swallowed up in victory.' This is a victory which is offered to all who turn to Jesus in faith. No one need be excluded from this victory. There need be no losers. The only loser is death itself. We are all invited to ask Paul's victorious question, 'Death, where is your victory? Death, where is your sting?' It is not surprising that this reading is often chosen by people to be read at funeral Masses. While taking the reality of death seriously for all of us, it is a wonderful proclamation that, because of Christ, death is not the end of the line, but the beginning of a new line. Death is the gateway to transformation, when our mortal nature puts on immortality, through our union with the risen Lord. We are not going nowhere. We are on a journey towards transformation; we wait in joyful hope for the Lord to come and transform these lowly bodies of ours into copies of his own glorious body.

Arising out of this glorious destination, Paul calls on us in that reading to never admit defeat, but to keep on working at the Lord's work always. Our ultimate destiny is beyond this life, but we are to take this life with the utmost seriousness. It is the time during which we work at the Lord's work. The other two readings today indicate to us what this involves. Jesus states in the gospel reading that a 'fully trained disciple will always be like the teacher'. Our calling is to be nothing less than a fully trained disciple, to be like our teacher, Jesus himself. Only then can we do the Lord's work. What was the Lord's work? Essentially, the Lord came to lead us to God. Our being like the Lord, like our teacher, involves us leading each other to God. If we lead each other to God we will certainly be working at the Lord's work.

The Lord does his work today of leading all people to God through his followers, his fully trained disciples.

The gospel reading suggests that if we are to lead each other to God, we need to be people of clear vision. As Jesus somewhat humorously asks at the beginning of the gospel reading, 'Can one blind man guide another? Surely both will fall into a pit?' We need to attend to the splinter or, indeed, the plank in our own eye before we can lead others anywhere. We need to be open to the likelihood that we have significant blind spots that inhibit our doing the Lord's work. It is one thing having blind points; it is more serious if we are blind to our blind spots. Acknowledging our blind spots is half the battle. In other words, a certain healthy self-criticism is needed if we are to relate in a life-giving way to others. We are probably all aware of a tendency in ourselves at times to be overly critical of others while failing to acknowledge our own failings. The business of trying to take the splinter out of someone else's eye while failing to notice the plank in our own is more than a humorous image. Jesus calls on us to be more preoccupied with the plank in our own eye than with the splinter in the eye of our neighbour. This is not an encouragement to naval gazing. Rather it is a call to the humble acknowledgement that we are not yet the fully trained disciples we are called to be. To use another image from the abundance of images in today's gospel reading, the store of goodness in our heart is not as full as it could be. What fills our hearts is not always the goodness of God. As the first reading suggests, it is often our conversation which reveals this to be the case.

Jesus declares that this kind of self-awareness is absolutely necessary if we are to lead others anywhere worthwhile. We cannot do the Lord's work, we cannot lead others to God, unless we are also aware of and, with the Lord's help, working on, our own blind spots.

Ninth Sunday in Ordinary Time

We know from experience that people can surprise us. We think we know someone or some group and we have expectations of them based on that understanding. However, people do not always live up to our expectations. They can fall below those expectations, leaving us disappointed, or they can behave above and beyond our expectations, leaving us amazed and delighted. We can be unpleasantly or pleasantly surprised by people. If we have been frequently disappointed by people in the course of our lives, it can be tempting to have low expectations of others. We can grow cynical and come to the point where we always expect to be let down by others. It is the attitude which says: 'He is very dependable; you can always depend on him to let you down.' If we get ourselves into that frame of mind, we run the risk of never allowing ourselves to be pleasantly surprised by others, even when there is good reason to be so. We can get into the mindset of Nathanael, 'Can anything good come out of Nazareth?' – with 'Nazareth' being anywhere and everywhere.

As followers of the Lord, we need to fight that tendency in ourselves whenever we notice it. This is not the mindset of Jesus, the one whom we claim to follow. He was always ready to be pleasantly surprised by others. He was open to and looked for the best in others, not the worst. In today's gospel reading, Jesus is pleasantly surprised by the attitude of a Roman centurion. Most Jews would have said, 'Can anything good come out of a Roman centurion?' Centurions were in the business of upholding Rome's occupation of Jewish soil. Yet, Jesus, a Jew, came to say of this centurion, 'I tell you, not even in Israel have I found faith like this.' Jesus could recognise that this traditional enemy had a deeper faith than he had found anywhere among his own people. Here was a Roman commanding officer who broke the mould, and Jesus was free to recognise this. Indeed, Jesus was not alone in being able to see the quality of this man; the Jewish leaders themselves said of him: 'He is friendly towards our people; in fact, he is the one who built the synagogue.' They too had allowed themselves to be pleasantly surprised by this official representative of the occupying power.

If Jesus and the Jewish leaders were 'astonished', in the good sense, at the faith of a Roman centurion, in the second reading we find Paul 'astonished', in the bad sense, at his Galatian converts. He is bitterly disappointed that they are abandoning the gospel that he preached to them and are in the process of embracing what Paul considers to be a perversion of the true gospel. Many of us will resonate with Paul's experience. People do let us down, all the time. We can carry within ourselves the wounds inflicted by the bitter experience of being let down, betrayed, abandoned, by those we had come to trust and love. Yet, the fact that we have had Paul's experience does not mean that we cannot have Jesus' experience too. We need to leave ourselves open to being pleasantly surprised by others because, as the letter to the Ephesians declares, the Lord's power 'at work within us is able to accomplish abundantly far more than all we can ask or imagine'. We can never underestimate how the Lord can work in our own lives or in the lives of others. We need to hold on to that conviction, especially when it comes to people that we find ourselves instinctively adverse to. One or two negative experiences of someone can be enough for us to write them off. We can be prone to forming negative opinions of some people before we have even met them. This is the attitude of Nathaniel, 'Can anything come out of Nazareth?' In his case, meeting Jesus of Nazareth was enough to kill off his prejudice. That can be the challenge for all of us. Can we allow the human encounter with someone to change the negativity we might instinctively feel towards them, for whatever reason? Can we see the good, especially when we are programmed to see the bad?

Today's gospel reading suggests that great goodness can be found where one least expects it. We need the freedom that Jesus showed in the gospel reading, the freedom to be astonished by those from whom we might have expected little. This is the freedom of the children of God. Such freedom is the fruit of the Holy Spirit in our lives. It is more likely to be given to those who, like the centurion, are aware of their own unworthiness to be in the Lord's presence.

Tenth Sunday in Ordinary Time

Many of us live our lives on the understanding that people should get only what they deserve. Indeed, a good deal of life operates on that basis, especially when it comes to our work life. People earn the salaries they receive, and if they work overtime they will receive a proportionately bigger pay check. Yet, we are only too well aware that the principle of people getting what they deserve or earn does not apply in many other areas of life. Although, in some respects, we can bring misfortune on ourselves, and it can be said that we get what we deserve, it more often appears to be the case that misfortune strikes people almost at random. At one point in the gospels, Jesus himself acknowledged as much when he asked, 'Those eighteen who were killed when the tower of Siloam fell on them – do you think they were worse offenders than all the others living in Jerusalem?' and then, immediately, answered, 'They were not, I tell you' (Lk 13:2-3). We can point to many such examples in our own time that give the lie to the notion that people get the misfortune they deserve.

It is equally true that many of the good things that come our way have not been earned or deserved by us. If we were to think about it, we would probably acknowledge that a great deal in our lives is pure gift. We unexpectedly meet someone that we have put no effort into finding, and that person becomes hugely significant for us and gives purpose and focus to our lives. After the rigours of winter, we take a walk in a park or gardens on a spring day and are overcome by the freshness of nature as it emerges from its winter slumber. We have done nothing to bring this about and, yet, there it is. We find ourselves going through a difficult time, for one reason or another, and the unsolicited thoughtfulness of a friend, relative or neighbour lifts our heart and helps us to keep going. In all sorts of ways, we can find ourselves unexpectedly graced and favoured.

The widow in today's gospel reading had such an experience of being surprisingly and marvellously graced. Having lost her husband, she now walked behind those who carried the body of her only son. She was alone in the world with no male provider. Moved by deep compassion for the woman's plight, Jesus restored life to the young man and gave him back alive to his mother. In last Sunday's gospel reading, Jesus responded to the request of the centurion for his seriously ill servant, a request which revealed a quality of faith that Jesus had not come across in the whole of Israel. However, in our reading this morning, there is no mention of any request made to Jesus by the distraught widow, and nothing is said about the woman's faith in Jesus. The likelihood is that Jesus was a complete stranger to her. Yet, Jesus graced this woman in an even more striking way than he had graced the centurion. He did not look for faith in her. Indeed, he appears to have had no expectations of her at all. She was wonderfully graced, and that was the beginning and end of it.

St Paul's experience of the risen Lord was not unlike the widow's experience of the earthly Jesus. Not only did Paul not have any faith in Jesus, but he was virulently opposed to Jesus and to all he stood for. He reminds the Galatians in today's second reading: 'You must have heard … how merciless I was in persecuting the church of God, how much damage I did to it.' Yet, for all his hostility to Jesus, Paul was extraordinarily graced by God, acknowledging in that same reading that 'God called me through his grace and chose to reveal his Son in me.' It was God's good pleasure to give Paul this wonderful gift, even though he had done nothing to deserve it and, indeed, had done a lot to suggest to some that he should not and could not have been graced in this way.

Both the experience of the widow and of Paul reveals something important about the Lord and how he relates to all of us. The Lord, out of his compassion and love, continually takes the initiative toward us, and his initiative appears to have little to do with any initiative, or lack of it, on our part. We can expect to be surprisingly graced by the Lord, because that is who and how he is. Whereas this does not leave us complacent in any way, it does keep us hopeful and expectant, especially in the face of our failings and struggles.

Eleventh Sunday in Ordinary Time

We know from our own experience that appearances can be deceptive. We buy something and when we get it home we discover it is not really all it was made out to be. Sometimes people are not always everything that they appear to be either. We can probably all think of high profile individuals whose public persona was subsequently shown not to correspond to the person they really were. This gap between image and reality is not, however, the prerogative of those who have a very public profile. We all recognise at times that the image people have of us can be somewhat flattering. We can be good at putting our best foot forward and disguising the other one. The reverse can also be the case. There can be more to some people than meets the eye. Sometimes it is only after someone dies that the good they did in the course of their lives becomes public knowledge. The public perception of some people can fall far short of the reality of their lives. A negative profile relating to one aspect of their lives can hide wonderful qualities that are much more defining of who they really are.

The two people who appear with Jesus in today's gospel reading were not all that they appeared to be. Simon the Pharisee was a respected religious leader who would have been regarded as more faithful to God's law than most. The public profile of the woman who was an uninvited guest at Simon's table was that of 'sinner', presumably because she had a known and verifiable reputation for breaking God's law. However, Jesus could see that in both their cases public perception did not correspond to the reality of their lives. Jesus recognised that Simon had omitted to show him the basic duties of hospitality, and that his perception of both Jesus and the woman was quite ungenerous. He doubted whether Jesus could be a prophet and he had no sense that there might be more to the woman than her bad name. In the words of Jesus, Simon 'showed little love'. Jesus also recognised that the woman, for all her reputation as a sinner, more than compensated for Simon's inhospitality by her extravagant gestures. Jesus had earlier conveyed to her that she was not merely a sinner but a forgiven sinner, and her lavish gestures of hospitality flowed from a heart that was bursting with gratitude. In contrast to Simon's 'little love' she showed 'great love'. Jesus holds up this woman to Simon as his teacher. 'Do you see this woman?' he said to Simon. It is as if Jesus was saying to Simon: 'Do not look on her merely as a sinner. Look more deeply and you will see that she has something to teach you and that you have a lot to learn from her.'

It is only in Luke's gospel that Jesus says in the context of the last supper: 'Who is greater, the one who is at the table or the one who serves? Is it not the one at the table? But I am among you as one who serves' (Lk 22:27). In today's gospel reading, Simon is 'the one at the table', the host, and the woman is the 'one who serves'. Her generous service of Jesus is a reflection of Jesus' generous service of us all. Like Jesus, she reveals the hospitality of God. Jesus saw much more of himself in her lavish gestures than in Simon's cautious restraint. He asks us all what he asks Simon, 'Do you see her?' We are all being asked to identify with this woman and to learn from her. One of the things we can learn from her is that public perception is not everything, and that those who rank poorly in human estimation can rank highly in God's estimation, and *vice versa*. She also teaches us that there is more to people than their mistakes and failures. Their can be a rush to demonise people today, especially high profile people, on the basis of some moral lapse or failure of duty. This becomes all that there is to say about the person, just as all that Simon had to say about the woman was that she had a bad name.

The woman also teaches us that in the words of the first letter of Peter, 'love covers a multitude of sins' (1 Peter 4:8). We probably all know of people who may not be 'religious' in the sense in which that word is often understood, but who show 'great love' by the generous way they serve others. Big hearted people who are lavish in their giving, like the woman in the gospel reading, reveal God to us in a very special way.

Twelfth Sunday in Ordinary Time

In the course of a day we can get asked any number of questions. We are walking along and someone pulls up in a car and asks us where a certain street is. We can be asked numerous questions in the course of a day relating to some area of work that we are very familiar with. Someone sits down in the evening to do a crossword and turns to us every now and then, asking us if we can interpret the clues. None of these kinds of questions make great demands on us or require too much thought. Occasionally, however, we can be asked questions that stop us in our tracks. As parents are well aware, children have a habit of asking questions that are more profound than they realise. 'Why don't the stars fall out of the sky?' 'Is there a heaven for cats?' The temptation can be to play for time and to kick for touch. One of our friends might ask us why something we do is so important to us. We may be well aware that it is important to us but we may never have really asked ourselves why that is so. Such question can leave us floundering for words.

In the gospel reading today, Jesus asks his disciples two questions that came straight out of his prayer. The first question was a relatively easy one: 'Who do the crowds say I am?' It is a question that can be easily answered by those who have their ear to the ground. The second question, however, was much more probing and challenging, because it was much more personal. He asked his disciples, 'But you, who do you say that I am?' We can almost imagine the disciples looking down at their toes. Thankfully, Peter came to everyone's rescue: 'The Christ of God', he said. Such an answer does not come off the top of the head. Peter had obviously given some thought to Jesus' identity. Peter's answer was a good answer, but it was not the full answer. Probing questions are not always answered at one go. We get a certain distance with our initial answer, but then we have to go back to the question and live with it for a little while longer before we can give a fuller answer. Jesus accepted Peter's answer, but he went on to answer his own question in a somewhat different way to how Peter had answered it. He spoke of himself, not as the Christ of God, but as the Son of Man who must suffer, be rejected, be put to death, before being raised up to new life. There was more to Jesus than even Peter, for all his insight, could possibly be aware of at that time.

Those of us who gather at this Eucharist this morning are in a better position than Peter was to answer Jesus' question. We have a sense of the whole story from Jesus' birth to Pentecost and beyond that Peter could not have had during Jesus' ministry. Yet, we cannot engage with this question like people who, having studied the whole course thoroughly from beginning to end, are supremely confident as we enter the examination hall. This is a question that still has the power to stop us in our tracks because it is not really asking us for information. It is asking us where we stand. In a way Jesus is asking us, 'Who am I for you?' 'What do I mean to you?' 'How committed are you to me and what I stand for?' 'Are you prepared to stand where I stand?'

To answer the question that Jesus asked, it is not enough to look into a text book. We have to look into our own hearts to answer it. We have to examine our values, our attitudes, our ways of behaving. It is there we will find the answer to the question, 'Who do you say I am?' Who we are, how we live, proclaims who Jesus is for us. It is no coincidence that having declared who he is, Jesus immediately goes on to declare who his disciples are. If he is the Son of Man who is ready to suffer and die, if that is necessary to remain faithful to God and to God's work, then his disciples are those who are prepared to take up their cross every day, when remaining faithful to his values and his message requires it. In that sense, the question Jesus asks of his disciples, 'Who do you say I am?' is essentially the question that, on another occasion, he asked two of the disciples, 'Are you able to drink the cup that I drink?' Here, indeed, is a question that cannot be answered lightly.

Thirteenth Sunday in Ordinary Time

This is the time of year when many people are preparing to set out on a journey, as they go off on their holidays. We always look forward to such journeys. They take us away from our normal place, our usual routine, and bring us to a different place where the routine is more relaxed. We set out on such journeys with a spring in our step. We sense that the journey ahead will renew and refresh us.

There are other journeys in life that we face into more reluctantly. We set out more because we have to than because we want to. We can all think of such journeys in our own lives. In times of sickness we often have to journey to hospital. We set out on that journey, trusting that it will be a healing one, but struggling to make the journey nonetheless. We might also think of times when we have to journey with someone we love who is seriously ill. We know we must travel this journey with them, even though it will cost us a lot. There are times in life when we feel we have no choice but to set out on what we know will be a difficult journey

The gospel reading describes Jesus facing into one such difficult journey, as he sets out for Jerusalem for the last time. This was a journey he knew he had to make and, yet, he was also aware that it would be the most difficult journey of his life. The word of God had to be proclaimed in Jerusalem, even though it had a reputation for killing the prophets. The gospel reading says that Jesus resolutely took the road for Jerusalem. He steeled himself for a journey that had to be made. No sooner had he set out on this journey than he experienced something of the rejection that awaited him in Jerusalem. A Samaritan village refused him hospitality. Here was an early reminder of worse to come. Yet, Jesus continued on his journey after that early set-back because, in the words of today's second reading, 'he was guided by the Spirit'. He made this difficult journey because the Spirit of God was directing him to take it, and he was completely open to the guidance of God's Spirit in his life. The path that the Spirit was prompting Jesus to take was one that would ultimately be life-giving for himself and for all who believe in him.

The Spirit of God in our lives will always be prompting us to take journeys that are life-giving for ourselves and for others. That path that leads to life will not always be an easy one. It will often be a path that brings us to our own Jerusalem on the way to that full life that God wants for us. There will often be a dying of some kind on the way to a fuller and more complete life. The temptation can be to take the path that looks easier, the path of, what Paul calls in the second reading, 'self indulgence'. The Spirit, however, will always direct us to take the path of self-giving rather than self-indulgence. If we are faithful to that path, it will be life-giving for ourselves and others. For Paul, true freedom, the freedom of the children of God, is to be found along this path. We can sometimes identify freedom with doing what we want, taking our own path. Paul reminds us that true freedom comes to those who do what God wants, who take the path that the Spirit prompts them to take. In that sense, Jesus was the freest human being who ever lived, because he was completely at the disposal of the Holy Spirit.

In some ways we can be like James and John in the gospel reading. In Galilee they left their nets to set out on a journey after Jesus. They took the path the Spirit prompted them to take. Yet, along the way they sometimes allowed a very different kind of spirit to influence them. In this morning's gospel they wanted to call fire down from heaven to destroy the Samaritans who had refused them hospitality. Such a violent response to the experience of rejection was not that of the Spirit, and Jesus rebuked them. We too have set out on a journey as followers of Jesus. Yet, like James and John, we can act and speak in a way that is inconsistent with the path we have taken. When that happens, as inevitably it will, we invite the Spirit of the Lord to come upon us afresh and to redirect our steps. With the Spirit's help, we once more set our face to go where the Lord is calling us to go.

Fourteenth Sunday in Ordinary Time

Helen Keller was born in the US towards the end of the 19th century, and she lived until the 1960s. In the first months of her life she fell ill, as a result of which she was left without hearing or sight for the rest of her life. Her speech was also severely impaired. Yet, with the help of a number of gifted people, including a woman called Ann Sullivan, Helen went on to become a great communicator. Anne worked hard to get Helen to identify objects she could touch by tracing the name of the object on Helen's hand. Eventually Helen began to build up a vocabulary in her head. She made great efforts to learn to speak, but her speech never really improved beyond the sounds that only Anne and others close to her could understand. Yet, Helen went on to write several books with Anne's help. After she time spent at College, she went on lecture tours, speaking of her experiences and beliefs to enthralled crowds, with Anne interpreting what she said, sentence by sentence.

Helen was once asked: 'If you had only one wish granted, what would you ask for?' Everyone believed that she would ask for the gift of sight or hearing for herself. Instead she replied simply, 'I would ask for world peace.' Her answer reveals a woman who was anything but self-absorbed. Given the restrictions under which she lived, she had good reason to be self-absorbed. Yet, she wanted not so much for herself but for others, especially for those who were suffering the effects of war and hostility.

The question, 'If you had only one wish granted, what would you ask for?' is one that has the potential to be very revealing. The way we answer that question can reveal a lot about us. It's a question that makes us reflect on what we value most deeply. I am reminded of the question that Jesus once asked James and John, 'What do you want me to do for you?' Another version of that question might be, 'What is your deepest prayer?' In this morning's gospel reading, Jesus suggests an appropriate prayer for his followers. He calls on the seventy-two to ask the Lord of the harvest to send labourers into his harvest.

Jesus suggests that an appropriate answer to the question, 'What is your one wish?' is that the Lord's harvest be gathered in, that the Lord's work be done. That is what we ask for at the beginning of the Lord's Prayer, when we pray: 'Your kingdom come, your will be done.' Jesus once said to his disciples, 'Seek first the kingdom of God.' For disciples of Jesus, the coming of God's kingdom is to be their primary wish, their deepest prayer. Peace, reconciliation between those who are hostile to each other, is one of the signs of the presence of God's kingdom. When Jesus sent out the seventy-two on mission, he told them that, on entering a house, they were to say: 'Peace to this house,' and 'The kingdom of God is very near to you.' The vision of peace flowing like a river towards Jerusalem, in today's first reading, is an image of God's kingdom. In contrast, the murder and mayhem that is happening in certain parts of the world today suggest the absence of God's kingdom.

The gospels, the church's teaching, and past and present experience, remind us strongly that there can be no peace without justice. When we pray, 'Your kingdom come,' we are asking not only for the coming of God's peace but, more fundamentally, for the coming of God's justice. Those who are labouring in the Lord's harvest will always be labouring for a peace that is the fruit of justice. That work of justice is adverted to in the gospel reading when Jesus calls on the seventy two to cure those who are sick. God's justice shows itself when the broken are made whole again, when, in that striking image of the first reading, people's bones flourish like grass and their hearts rejoice, or, in the words of Paul in the second reading, when we become altogether new creatures.

The gospel reading suggests that we each have a role to play in bringing about God's justice and peace. Anne Sullivan's presence to Helen Keller allowed Helen to flourish and her heart to rejoice. Her involvement with Helen enabled her to become an altogether new creature. Each of us in our own way can have such a role in the life of others. As we ask the Lord of the harvest to send labourers into his harvest, we also make ourselves available as labourers in that harvest. We invite the Lord to work through us in healing and life-giving ways.

Fifteenth Sunday in Ordinary Time

When individuals or groups are in conflict, it can be difficult for the conflicting parties to see any good in each other. In times of war, in particular, the warring parties often demonise each other. In the case of the current Israeli-Palestinian conflict, for example, it is probably very difficult for many Palestinians to bring together the noun 'Jew' and the adjective 'good', and equally difficult for many Jews to associate the noun 'Palestinian' with the adjective 'good'. A pastor working in the Middle East confessed that never once was he even tempted to tell Palestinians a story about a noble Israeli. However, Jesus does the equivalent of that in today's gospel reading. We have become used to referring to the story Jesus tells as the parable of the good Samaritan. We can forget that, in the Jewish world of Jesus, the words 'good' and 'Samaritan' would never have been found together.

After stating that the priest and the Levite passed by the broken traveller, his listeners were probably expecting that Jesus would then go on to say that a Jewish layman came along and did the decent thing. The story would then have had an anti-clerical tone, and it would have been appreciated as such. However, the story turned out to be much more subversive than that. It was not a Jewish lay person who responded to the broken traveller, but a despised Samaritan. A member of the group traditionally demonised by Jews showed what keeping God's law really meant in practice. When the Jewish lawyer was asked by Jesus, 'Which of the three do you think proved himself to be a neighbour?' he could not bring himself to say 'the Samaritan'. He simply said, 'The one who showed compassion.'

The story Jesus told, like all his parables, can be heard at many levels. We can hear it as a reminder to us that those we are tempted to dismiss and look down on can often teach us what it means to live as God intends us to live. The Samaritan in the parable was an image of Jesus – just as Jesus is an image of God, as Paul reminds us in today's second reading. In drawing a picture of the compassionate response of the Samaritan to the wounded traveller, Jesus was drawing a picture of his own compassionate ministry. The parable indicates that Jesus figures can

be found in unexpected places. It invites us to recognise goodness among those we are prone to dismiss or reject.

The parable also reminds us that help can come to us from
unexpected quarters. The wounded man in the parable was pre-
sumable a Jew. He would not have expected help to come from a
Samaritan. At crucial moments we too can receive help from
people we would not have expected to help us. In our hour of
need we can discover that our assessment of someone was far
too ungenerous. The parable suggests that God can sometimes
come to us in unfamiliar guises, that his compassionate love can
be revealed to us by the outsider, the one we would normally
have considered alien to us. When people with whom we are at
odds reach out in us in our hour of need, we can be tempted to
keep them at bay. The Jewish lawyer struggled to accept that
God's compassionate presence could be revealed through the
despised Samaritan. The parable calls on us to allow God to
come to us in and through those of God's own choosing.

In the story of the good Samarian we might be inclined at
times to identify with the half-dead traveller. Life has a way of
leaving us half-dead at times. We might need to pray for the
freedom to accept God's compassion from whatever direction it
comes. Yet today's parable more directly invites us to identify
with the Samaritan. What Jesus said to the lawyer, he says to us
all: 'Go, and do the same yourself.' We all have the potential to
make tangible God's compassionate presence to others. The first
step in doing that is to notice. It is first said of the Samaritan that
he saw the traveller, he noticed him. Noticing is a small but very
significant first step. Yet, it is not enough. The priest and the
Levite also noticed, they too saw. What distinguished the
Samaritan from them was that he allowed himself to be deeply
moved by what he saw. Compassion involves that deep inner
movement which comes from allowing ourselves to experience
something of the pain of the other. That inner movement will
lead to some form of outer movement, some appropriate action
on behalf of the other. Such action, according to the gospel reading, is the path to life, for the other and for ourselves.

Sixteenth Sunday in Ordinary Time

One of the great gifts we can give each other is the gift of our attention. We tend to be very aware when people are paying attention to us and when they are not. It can be disconcerting to find ourselves saying something to someone and then to get a response which indicates that the person has not really heard us. On the other hand, we value very much those who attend to us when we have something to say, especially if they are capable of noticing not only the words we speak but what is going on within us which our words may only be partially expressing.

Real attention goes beyond listening to the words someone might be speaking; it involves attending to the whole person. Being truly attentive to someone will express itself in a variety of ways. Sometimes it will involve very careful listening. At other times it will require activity on our part. A good example of this latter kind of attentiveness was the Samaritan in last Sunday's gospel reading. When he noticed the broken traveller on the roadside, he attended to him by jumping into action: bandaging his wounds, pouring oil and wine on them, lifting him on his own mount, carrying him to the inn, looking after him there, handing over money to the innkeeper and promising to visit on his way back. Here, indeed, was a marvellous quality of attention. We find something similar in today's first reading. In response to the arrival of the three guests, Abraham jumps into action: running to meet them, hastening to his wife Sarah to give her instructions for the meal, running to take a calf from his flock, giving it to the servant to prepare, placing the prepared calf along with cream and milk before the visitors. Both the frenetic activity of the Samaritan and of Abraham are model responses to people in need, be it the need of healing in the first instance or of hospitality in the second.

We all need the kind of attention from time to time that the Samaritan and Abraham provided. Every so often, we need people to go into overdrive for us – especially when it might be a case of life or death, as in the story of the Samaritan. However, we also know from experience that there are times when we need a different kind of attention, which does not involve someone 'doing' something for us, taking all kinds of initiatives on our behalf. Indeed, it can be somewhat annoying when, for example, a good friend starts doing things for us that we don't want done or need doing, when all we really want is their presence. There are different forms of hospitality; there is the hospitality of activity and the hospitality of presence. In today's gospel reading, Martha exemplifies the hospitality of activity and Mary the hospitality of presence. It seems that on this occasion, it was the hospitality of presence rather than of activity that Jesus sought. In that sense, Mary read the situation better than Martha; she chose the better part. Jesus was not looking for an elaborate meal; he had something to say and it was Mary who noticed this and sat at his feet to listen to his word. Mary was more hospitable on this occasion because she was more attentive to the guest than Martha was. There is a time to listen and there is a time to get busy. As the Book of Qoheleth puts it, 'for everything there is a season, and a time for every matter under heaven'. Wisdom consists in knowing what is appropriate at any particular time.

In our own relationship with the Lord there is a time for both sitting at his feet to listen to him and for rolling up our sleeves and getting down to some serious work. We need to attend to both the Lord of the work and the work of the Lord. The Lord needs us at times to be the good Samaritan to others, to share in his work of bringing good news to the poor and proclaiming release to captives. There are other times when he needs us and wants us to be still before him and to ponder his word. This is the two-fold rhythm that is at the heart of following him. In these busy times, it can be the rhythm of listening to his word in prayerful silence that can get neglected. We have something to learn from Mary, as much as from Abraham. If we learn from both, we will be like the seed that fell on good soil, those who 'hearing the word, hold it fast in an honest and good heart, and bring forth fruit in patience' (Lk 8:15).

Seventeenth Sunday in Ordinary Time

Most of us will have had various teachers in the course of our lives. We might feel that many of them made little impression on us. Others may have left an impression on us for the wrong reasons! Hopefully there will be some that we recall with great affection and appreciation because we are aware that they passed on to us something very valuable. They set us on a path that proved to be of enormous benefit to ourselves and to others. When we think back on those particular teachers and ask why they impressed us, we might find that it was about more than just the actual content of their teaching. It also had to do with their enthusiasm for their subject. They were clearly in love with their subject and they succeeded in communicating something of that love to us. Another reason for the impact they made on us may have had to do with how they related to us. They took us seriously; they treated us with respect. They shared their knowledge and love of their subject with us because they knew it would serve us well as human beings.

A good teacher in this sense is likely to be in demand; people will approach such people and call on them to teach. This is what we find happening in this morning's gospel reading. The disciples approach Jesus and ask him to teach them how to pray. They had come to recognise him as a good teacher. In particular, they had become very aware that here was someone who knew something about God and, even more so, who knew and loved God personally. They had seen him communicate with God while at prayer. Shortly before the disciples made this request, Luke tells us that 'at that same hour, Jesus rejoiced in the Holy Spirit and said, "I thank you, Father, Lord of heaven and earth…"'(Lk 10:21). The disciples wanted to be able to communicate with God as Jesus did, to share in some way in his own relationship with God. Like any good teacher, Jesus responded to their request. Teachers are communicators who want to share what they have come to learn. Jesus passionately wanted to share his relationship with God, to bring others into that relationship. He was not a hoarder who kept what he had to himself. As we find him saying in the gospel of John: 'I have spoken openly to the world … I have always taught in synagogues and in the temple. I have said nothing in secret' (Jn 18:19). In response to the disciples' request, Jesus gave them an actual prayer which is also a teaching on how to pray.

A good teacher will not only give concrete information but in so doing will also communicate a way of approaching the subject so that pupils can go off and apply this approach creatively for themselves. Jesus was saying to his disciples: Here is a prayer and here is also an approach to prayer. We pray the prayer that has become known as the Lord's Prayer every time we gather to celebrate the Eucharist and on other occasions of liturgical and personal prayer. We have taken the prayer, but we also need to absorb the approach to prayer that this prayer expresses.

Jesus invites us to address God in the same intimate way as he did, as 'Abba, Father' and he empowers us to do so by sending us the Holy Spirit. As Paul writes to the Galatians, 'God has sent the Spirit of his Son into our hearts, crying "Abba, Father!"' (Gal 4:6). In this prayer, Jesus teaches us that our primary focus in prayer is to be on God rather than on ourselves. To pray is to go out of ourselves towards God. We express our longing for God's name to be honoured, for God's kingdom to come, for God's will to be done. In prayer we try to identify with God's purpose, whatever that might be, and even when we do not fully understand it.

Within that primary focus, there is also scope for a focus on ourselves, but not so much on ourselves as individuals but as a community of believers. After the opening two petitions which have to do with God, the concluding petitions have to do not with 'me' but with 'us'. Together we pray to God out of our shared needs. We all need daily sustenance, the strength to keep going, especially when life is a struggle. We all need God's forgiveness and the freedom to pass that forgiveness on others. We all need God to stand with us when our faith is being put to the test. In some ways, all genuine prayer will be shaped by these concerns of the Lord's Prayer.

Eighteenth Sunday in Ordinary Time

The making of a will is one of the important acts of adulthood. We can be rather reluctant to sit down and make our will. To do so is to acknowledge in a very concrete way that we are mortal, that one day we will leave our possessions to others. The author of the book of Qoheleth saw this as part of the meaninglessness of life – 'a person who has laboured ... must leave what is his own to someone who has not toiled for it at all'. Yet, there can be great meaning in the act of leaving what is our own to those who have not laboured for it. The decisions we make in regard to our possessions will speak volumes about who and what we really value in life. Our will is a statement of our loves and passions, our values and interests.

When a will is not made or when it is unclear, trouble very often ensues, as family members attempt to interpret what the deceased person really intended. Non-family members can get drawn into the family quarrel. In the gospel reading today, someone tries to draw Jesus into a family dispute about inheritance. A man comes up to Jesus and says, 'Master, tell my brother to give me a share of our inheritance.' Wisely, Jesus does not get involved in this family dispute. Instead, he seizes on this man's request to warn against the dangers of greed. Greed is the desire to acquire more than we need or is good for us. When we give in to greed we invariably do damage not only to ourselves but to others as well. Parents instinctively tell their children not to be greedy when they see them taking more than they need, thereby depriving others. However, greed is more an adult issue than a childhood one.

Jesus holds up children as models of how to receive the kingdom of God. He tells his own disciples: 'Truly I tell you, whoever does not receive the kingdom of God as a little child will never enter it.' Jesus suggests that children very often have the open hands and the open hearts that are needed to receive God's presence and to respond to God's call. In the gospel reading this morning, Jesus tells a story of a greedy adult who stands at the opposite end of the spectrum to the responsive child. Here is a man whose hands are not open because they have a tight grip on what he owns, and whose heart is not open because it is full of anxiety about the safe storage of all he possesses. You could say that he is full of himself. It is striking that he is the only person to inhabit the story that Jesus tells. There is no room there for anyone else. When he speaks, he speaks to himself; his words have to do with himself: 'my crops, my barns, my grain, my goods, my soul'.

You could say that the man in the parable had lost a sense of proportion. The value he placed on his possessions was out of proportion to their real value. Greed, by definition, gets things out of proportion, driving us to invest ourselves in what is of minor value and in the process making us miss what is of real value. We can all get things out of proportion. We can allow something to become supremely important for us, even though in the greater scheme of things, it is not so important. Jesus constantly points us towards what is of ultimate value. His life shows us what it means to be 'rich in the sight of God', in the words of the gospel reading. His was a generous life; he gave generously on behalf of others. Because of his generous love, he was supremely rich in the sight of God. When we allow the risen Jesus to live out his generosity in and through us, we too become rich in the sight of God. In the words of today's second reading, we become renewed in the image of our creator.

The antithesis of greed is generosity. The antithesis of the man in today's parable is the poor widow who placed everything she had into the temple treasury, 'all she had to live on'. We can all think of generous people like her, those who give generously of themselves to others, whether it is of their time, their energy, their resources, their possessions. We know we have been enriched by such people. Those who are rich in the sight of God truly enrich the lives of others. We pray that by the time the Lord calls us to himself at the end of our lives, we too will have become rich in the sight of God.

Nineteenth Sunday in Ordinary Time

The sudden death of someone we are close to is always a very difficult experience. Sudden death has a way of putting things in perspective. It brings home to us that human life is fragile. Although we have to live our lives on the basis that we will be alive tomorrow and next week and next month, we cannot be sure we will be. Even though human beings are more in control of their lives and of their environment than they ever have been in human history, yet, unless we take our own life, we have no control over when we will die.

For those of us who have faith in Christ, our perspective on death, whether it is our own death or the death of those close to us, is the perspective of God. Something of that perspective is to be found in today's readings. The second reading from the letter to the Hebrews reminds us that for us as Christians, life is a journey towards our heavenly homeland. It speaks of believers as nomads on earth. The nomad in the Middle East travelled from place to place in constant search of water and pasture for his flock. He never settled in any one place for long. In speaking of people of faith as nomads on earth, the second reading reminds us that this earth is not our final resting place; it can never be our final home. That is not to say that we do not take seriously this earth and everything and everybody on it, or that we devalue this earth or flee from it as if it were harmful. However, it is to say that in living on this earth we always look beyond it, as the nomad in the desert was always looking beyond wherever he and his flock happened to be. The second reading says that even when, after a long journey, Abraham reached the promised land, he did not consider this to be the end of his journey. Rather, he looked forward to a city founded, designed and built by God.

This is the perspective of faith. In the words of that same reading, we look towards realities that at present remain unseen. Even though these realities remain unseen, our faith assures us of their existence. Indeed, because of our faith, there is a sense in which we already possess the things we hope for. Our faith relationship with the Lord gives us a foretaste, an anticipation of eternal life. Sometimes we might feel that our faith is weak; we can be assailed by doubts of all kinds. Indeed, our faith needs to be nurtured and nourished. We do this above all through prayer. Our faith increases every time we pray. Prayer is spending time with God and the more time we spend with someone the more we get to know them. The more we pray the more we get to know God. Since faith is knowing God, the more we pray, the deeper our faith. God always increases our faith whenever we pray. Our praying can take many different forms. We can pray with words, and we can pray without any words at all. When we pray with words, we can use our own words or set words, either from a book or that we know by heart.

The more we pray, the more our faith increases and the more our perspective on this life becomes God's perspective. We come to see this life as a journey during which we seek to live in a way that is worthy of those who one day will live forever in God's presence. We will want to live in a way that leaves us ready for that moment when, in the image of today's gospel reading, the master of the house comes and knocks on our door. When he comes, we would like him to find us dressed for action, with our lamps lit. When the Lord knocks, we would hope to be people who are clothed with Christ, who have been shaped by Christ's values, in whom the Spirit of Christ is alive, in whom the flame of Christ that was lit at our baptism continues to burn brightly. In other words, our journey through this life is one in which we gradually allow Christ to live out his life more fully in us.

The gospel reading assures us that if the master finds us like this when he comes and knocks, he will become our servant. In an extraordinary role reversal, the Lord of the universe will put on an apron, sit us down at table and wait on us. We will be honoured guests at the banquet of eternal life, and the one we have been serving will become our servant.

Twentieth Sunday in Ordinary Time

Very few of us relish confrontation. We like to be on good terms with people and we like people to be on good terms with us. The quiet life holds an attraction for us. We are tempted by the goal of peace at any price. Yet, there have always been people who cannot live their lives on that basis. They will cause a stir whenever certain values are being undermined, such as the value of justice, of truth, of the protection of the most vulnerable. They will stick their neck out and risk bringing trouble on themselves because their commitment to these values is stronger than their desire for a tension free life. We need such people to prevent us from becoming too complacent.

In the gospel reading this morning we have one of those sayings of Jesus that can pull us up short and make us stop and think. He declares that he has come not to bring peace on earth but, rather, division. What are we to make of this? Does the fourth gospel not present us with a Jesus who says, 'Peace I leave with you, my peace I give to you' (Jn 14:27) and does not that gospel tell us that, far from coming to create division, Jesus died to gather together the scattered children of God (Jn 11:52)? Yet, the saying of Jesus this morning is true of what actually happened within families. Those members of families who became disciples of Jesus and embraced his vision and his teaching often found themselves at odds with other family members who refused to take that step. Turning to the fourth gospel again, you might remember the story of the man born blind. When, subsequent to his healing, he went on to declare himself for Jesus and all Jesus stood for, his own parents disowned him to the religious leaders of the time, and he was thrown out of the synagogue (Jn 9:20-23, 34).

Jesus did not come with the explicit intention of dividing people or families. He came to proclaim the kingdom of God, the values that God holds dear and wants us to live by. The consequences of proclaiming those values by his word and deed were that communities and families ended up divided. Peace or unity at any price was not what Jesus was about. We might be inclined to think: 'Well that was then and this is now.' Yet, the Jesus who lived and worked two thousand years ago is the same risen Lord who lives and works among us today, and the world in which we live today is as resistant to the gospel as it was when Jesus first proclaimed it. We can expect that if we try to live by the values of the gospel today, we will find ourselves at odds with people who have a different set of values. There can be enormous peer pressure, especially on young people, to take a very different path to the one that Jesus calls us to take. The refusal to swim with the tide, to do what everyone is doing, can evoke ridicule and hostility from others, leaving people quite isolated. Like Jeremiah in the first reading we can find ourselves thrown into a muddy well. Jesus himself in today's gospel reading speaks about the great distress he continues to experience until his mission is completed. We can expect to share in his distress, his dis-ease, if we commit ourselves to him and identify with his way.

Because living the gospel and being wholehearted in our following of the Lord will never be easy and will always be counter-cultural to some degree, we cannot travel this path on our own. We need support, what the second reading refers to as 'many witnesses ... on every side of us'. We need the witness of each other if, in the words of that reading, we are to 'keep running steadily in the race that we have started'. The effort that any one of us makes to be true to the gospel is a support for everyone else. The failure of any one of us to live the gospel makes it more difficult for the rest of us to do so.

As well as needing the witness of each other, that second reading also tells us that we must 'not loose sight of Jesus who leads us in our faith and brings it to perfection'. Not only is the journey of faith one we travel together, we have a leader on this journey, someone who is out there ahead of us and who has already travelled this journey for us. We need to keep him in focus, listening to his word, celebrating his presence in the Eucharist, conversing with him in prayer.

Twenty-First Sunday in Ordinary Time

Few of us would like to be thought of as 'narrow minded'. In a society where 'broad-mindedness' is celebrated, narrowness of mind is looked down upon. We associate it with bigotry and a lack of imagination, whereas the broad minded person is considered tolerant and open.

Yet in today's gospel, the Lord states that, when it comes to our eternal salvation, a certain kind of narrow-mindedness is needed: 'Try your best to enter by the narrow door.' Jesus was responding to a question put to him by someone in the crowd, 'Sir, will there be only a few saved?' Rather than getting into an unhelpful discussion about how many will be saved, Jesus challenged those travelling with him to strive to enter by the narrow door. The invitation to 'strive' suggests struggle and exertion. Jesus suggests that taking the path that leads through the narrow door requires effort and determination. To get through a narrow door you need a clear vision of where you are going and a certain commitment to get there. Jesus reminds us that those who wish to be his followers need all these qualities of commitment, clarity of vision, focus, and determination.

Becoming one of the Lord's followers is never a laid-back affair. It requires a conscious and deliberate effort on our part. Much of the culture in which we live today pulls us in very different directions to the one the gospel calls us to take. There can be a lot of pressure on people, some of it subtle, to act in ways that are contrary to the message of Jesus. We need to be very deliberate about the living of our faith in today's world. Otherwise, we will be pulled in other directions. At some point in our lives, we need to make our own the decision that our parents once made for us when they brought us to the church for baptism. Some people argue that you should allow children to make their own decision about baptism, when they are old enough to do so. However, if we believe that baptism into Christ, with all that goes with it, is really worthwhile, we will want children to receive this wonderful gift early in life. Yet, it is important that as the child grows towards adulthood he or she says their own 'yes' to this gift and to all it implies. Baptism opens a door for us, but we then have to strive to enter through that door. Baptism calls on us to keep on entering through the door that is Jesus, to walk in his way, to follow his lead. This will always require on-going effort and alertness on our part.

Yet, we need to keep reminding ourselves that it is not all down to our own striving. Our effort is contained within the Lord's effort on our behalf. The Lord is always drawing us through that narrow door that leads to life. He is not standing on the far side of the door looking at our efforts in some kind of de-tached way. In the first reading, the Lord, speaking through the prophet Isaiah, states: 'I am going to gather the nations of every language.' The door may be narrow, but the Lord is going to pull through that door large numbers from every language and culture. Even though the door is narrow, there is nothing nar-row about the huge, diverse gathering that assembles beyond it. In the gospel reading, Jesus speaks of people from east and west, north and south who take their place at the feast on the far side of the narrow door in the kingdom of God. There is an implicit answer here to the question that was put to Jesus in the gospel reading, 'Will only a few be saved?' The answer to that question is 'no'. People from the four corners of the earth will get through that door, and some of those who get through may surprise us, 'those now last will be first'.

The efforts we have to make to get through the narrow door, therefore, are never anxious, despairing efforts. They are the ef-forts of those who know that the Lord's efforts on our behalf are always much greater than our efforts on his behalf. We keep on striving in the conviction that, in the words of today's psalm, 'strong is the Lord's love for us; he is faithful for ever'. It is true that we cannot be presumptuous, like those in the gospel read-ing who said: 'We once ate and drank in your company, you taught in our streets.' Yet, we can be confident that if we rely on the Lord's help, while making every effort we can, he will see us through the narrow gate.

Twenty-Second Sunday in Ordinary Time

The giving of medals is the traditional way of honouring achievement in the field of sport. When a married couple reach 40 or 50 years of married life, the achievement will be celebrated with some kind of social event, during which the couple will be honoured and congratulated. Significant birthdays are honoured in similar ways.

It is important that we take time to honour people who are deserving of honour. In the gospel reading Jesus is critical of those who seek out honour for themselves. At the meal to which he had been invited, he noticed how some of the guests went out of their way to pick places of honour. In response, Jesus speaks a parable that is critical of this kind of self-promoting behaviour. Jesus suggests that his followers should not be concerned about seeking honour from others. What really matters is the honour we will receive from God. We are to live in such a way that God will honour and exalt us. God's honouring of us may not happen in this life. However, if we live in a way that is shaped by the gospel, God will certainly honour us after death. As Jesus says in the gospel reading, repayment will be made when the virtuous rise again. The extent to which God honours all those who do God's will is beautifully expressed in today's second reading. God will bring us to the heavenly Jerusalem, where we will have citizenship alongside the millions of angels who have gathered there and the spirits of the saints who have been made perfect.

The readings today suggest that this is the only honour worth waiting for. The various honours we might receive in this life fade into insignificance compared to the honour that God wants to confer on us. That is why as followers of Jesus we are not to be concerned as to whether or not the good that we do is recognised by others. Our only concern is to live as Jesus calls us to live, as God intends us to live. We do not worry about recognition for that from others. That is not to say that we do not welcome it graciously if it is given. However, if it does not come, it makes no difference to how we live our lives, because what really matters to us is the honour we will receive from God.

It can be tempting to be less generous in our way of living if appreciation is not forthcoming. We might be inclined to give up some worthwhile work we are doing for others if that work is not recognised. This is a temptation to be resisted. The Lord calls on us to be faithful to the good we are doing, even when we are not recognised. The supreme example of this approach to life is Jesus himself. He was faithful to his God-given mission even when it brought him dishonour. There was nothing more dishonourable than death by crucifixion. Yet, in spite of the dishonour that it brought him, Jesus was faithful to the work that God gave him to do. Jesus knew that beyond the very dishonouring experience of crucifixion, he would be honoured by God. As Paul reminds us, God highly exalted him, and gave him a name that is beyond all names.

We can probably all think of people in our own experience who go about doing good in a quiet way, without looking for reward or favour in return. They work away in season and out of season, irrespective of whether they are given recognition or not. They are not in the business of giving in order to receive something back. They are not like those that Jesus refers to in the gospel reading who invite others to a meal so that they might get an invitation in return. In contrast, Jesus encourages us to give to those who are not in a position to give us anything in return. We are to serve others, not for what we might receive back from them, but because it is the right thing to do, because it is what the Lord is asking of us. We leave it to the Lord to honour us in his own way and in his own time, even if such honour lies beyond this life, as often it will. It is difficult to live in this way without some element of prayer in our lives. In prayer we receive from the Lord the strength to be faithful, regardless of how our efforts are responded to. Jesus' prayer in the garden of Gethsemane kept him faithful as he faced into his dishonourable death. In prayer, we learn how to wait on the honour that only the Lord can give.

Twenty-Third Sunday in Ordinary Time

We know from experience how difficult it can be to understand what is going on in someone else's mind and heart. We can find ourselves wondering why someone acts in the way he or she does. This can be true even when the person is someone we are close to. To some extent, each of us can also be something of a mystery to ourselves. We can find ourselves wondering why we said or did something. We can use an expression like, 'I don't know what got into me', admitting that, at least on that occasion, we were something of a stranger to ourselves.

The first reading from the Book of Wisdom acknowledges this, remarking on how hard it is to work out what is on earth, and how laborious it is to know what lies within our reach. The conclusion that the author draws from this is, how much more difficult must it be to know the intentions of God and to understand the will of the Lord. If what is within our reach is hard to fathom, who can discover what is in the heavens?

Yet, in the matter of understanding the intentions of God, we have not been left to our own devices. God has made it possible for us to know God's intentions and to understand God's will. As the first reading declares, God has given us wisdom and sent his Holy Spirit from above. Christ has come among us as the Wisdom of God, revealing God's will to us. Both God the Father and Christ his Son have poured the Holy Spirit into our hearts, and that Spirit enlightens us about God's intentions and will. As we try to discern what God is asking of us, we can look to his Son and we can invoke the Holy Spirit.

In our lives, we can find ourselves dealing with complex situations that we could never have anticipated. Knowing what God is asking of us in those situations can be difficult. We often need to take time to reflect and pray, so as to allow God the opportunity to give us the help that only God can give. In the gospel reading, Jesus tells two parables which emphasise the importance of sitting down and thinking something through, rather than rushing into something, and discovering too late that the wrong path has been taken. Jesus suggests in those parables that if we are to take the path that God wants us to take, we need to be reflective and prayerful about what we are doing. We need to turn to God's Son and ask him to fill us with his wisdom; we need to open our hearts to God's Spirit from on high.

Although we live in an age where self-sufficiency is highly valued, when it comes to our relationship with God, we are never self-sufficient. We are always beggars. If we are to discover the path that God is asking us to take, we will always need the help that God alone makes available to us.

The gospel reading suggests that the path that God calls us to take will often prove to be the more difficult path. Jesus travelled God's path and it brought him to the cross. For us, too, taking the path God is calling us to take may mean the cross. It may involve, for example, finding ourselves at odds with family, friends and peers. We may know what path God is asking us to take, but we can hesitate to take that path if the price we have to pay is loss of standing among those who are important to us.

This was the situation in which Philemon found himself in today's second reading. His runaway slave, Onesimus, had met up with Paul, and was converted by Paul to the Christian faith. Paul was now sending Onesimus back to his former master, asking him to receive Onesimus back, no longer as a slave but as a brother in Christ, as an equal. In responding to Paul's request, Philemon stood to loose a great deal, because his peers would not have looked kindly on this practice of runaway slaves being welcomed back as equals. Yet, this was the difficult path the Lord was asking Philemon to take.

We can all find ourselves in a similar situation to Philemon. We can be faced with a difficult path, which we know in our heart of hearts is the one God wants us to take. We may find ourselves hesitating to take it. It is then, above all, that we need to give ourselves time to call on the resources that the Lord makes available to us. In such moments, we can be assured that our prayer will not go unanswered.

Twenty-Fourth Sunday in Ordinary Time

I am sure that most of us are familiar with the experience of loss. The most painful experience of loss is undoubtedly when someone close to us dies. Who among us has not shed bitter tears at the death of a mother, father, spouse, brother, sister, son, daughter, or very dear friend. Then there are the many other losses that life inevitably brings. Because of illness or the aging process we loose some of our dynamism and energy; we experience the frustration of not being able to do what we once did. Even in our younger years we will often have to deal with loss. A friendship we had great hopes for dies away; a goal we had set ourselves is never reached. We are left with a sense of what might have been.

The three stories that Jesus tells in the gospel reading have the experience of loss at their centre. A shepherd losses one of his sheep, a woman one of her coins, a father one of his sons. The experience of loss generated great energy in each of these three people. The shepherd went out into the hills after his lost sheep; the woman swept her little house diligently for her lost coin; the father scanned the horizon daily for his lost son. Many people could identify with that energetic response to the experience of loss. If a child goes missing parents will drop everything to search. Those who are close to the family will do the same. The search becomes all consuming. Everything else is put aside.

The son who went missing in today's gospel reading was not a child. He was a young adult who freely decided to get lost. Yet, the father searched for this adult son as passionately as if he was a child who had inadvertently gone missing. Spotting the son while he was still a long way off suggests that the father had been daily scanning the horizon in hope. While respecting his son's freedom to leave home, his father never left his son. He continued to carry his son in his mind and heart. The father's love for the son did not grow cold, even in the face of his son's self-centred decision to leave home.

As we read this story, we sense that this is a special father. Jesus presented this father figure as an image of God. Jesus was telling us that God seeks us out with a passion, and that God holds onto to us even when we let go of God. God's way of relating to us is not dependant on our way of relating to God. Here indeed is good news for those who, in their heart of hearts, know that they have sinned against heaven and against their fellow human being; here indeed is good news for all of us, because we all belong in that group.

When telling this story, Jesus was presenting the father as an image of God, but he was also presenting the father as an image of what we can all become. When we read this story, we might find it difficult to identify with the father. We sense that the gap between how the father behaves and how we behave is too great. We are aware of how we often treat others as they treat us, trading hurt for hurt, rejection for rejection. We know our tendency to turn our backs on those who have turned their backs on us, even if they belong within our own family circle. Yet, our reluctance to identify with the father may indicate that God is speaking to us through this story. God may be calling us to become that father figure for someone in our lives. God may be asking us to open the doors of our hearts to someone we may have turned our back on, perhaps for good reasons, but who is now trying to find a way back to us.

If we find it difficult to identify with the father in the story, we may find it correspondingly easy to identify with the elder son. His anger at the welcome given to his brother, whom he considered a waster, is a response we have a sneaking sympathy for. Somehow, we know this character of the elder brother all too well, as well as we know ourselves, perhaps. If the father's response to the younger son speaks to us of God, the response of the older brother speaks to us of ourselves. The call the parable makes on us is to move from the response of the elder brother to that of the father, to move from anger towards compassion. This can be a difficult journey, but it is one we can travel with the Lord's help.

Twenty-Fifth Sunday in Ordinary Time

Different people will react to a crisis situation in different ways. Some people tend to go to pieces. They feel overwhelmed by the crisis and sink down under it. Then there are others who are at their best in a crisis. They stay calm and get clarity as to the best course of action to take. Such people tend to have a steadying influence on everyone else.

The main character in this morning's gospel reading seems to have belonged in that second group. A steward of a wealthy farmer was suddenly catapulted into a crisis situation. He found himself facing immediate unemployment, without today's safety net of social welfare assistance. As he stared into the abyss, he took resolute action to secure his future. Although what he did was morally suspect – arbitrarily reducing the debt owed by his boss's clients – it gained him the friendship of others at a time when he was very vulnerable. Surprisingly, his decisive action won the praise of his boss for its cleverness, even though the boss was going to lose out because of it.

This story in today's gospel reading is probably the strangest parable in all of the gospels. It comes immediately after the parable of the prodigal son that we heard last Sunday. Unlike that parable, there are really no attractive characters in the parable we have just heard. Neither the rich man nor his steward is a particularly praiseworthy person. Yet, Jesus told this story to his disciples, presumably because he recognised that it had something to teach them. Perhaps we are being reminded that God can speak to us through all sorts of people, including those who have something of the rogue about them. Jesus is telling us that God communicates with us through all of life's situations, including those situations that are not particularly noble.

Jesus wanted his disciples to learn something from the way that the steward coped with a crisis situation in his life. The steward was very resourceful in securing his own future when that future appeared to be very bleak. Jesus wants his followers to be equally resourceful in securing God's future. The steward was on the ball when it came to looking out for his own interests. The parable suggests that as followers of Jesus we need to be equally on the ball when it comes to looking out for God's interests. Jesus implies that the qualities that the steward displayed in a crisis will also be very necessary in the service of God's kingdom – in particular, his sense of urgency, his decisiveness, his imagination. If God's kingdom is to come, the followers of Jesus will need all of these qualities. We cannot wait for God to do everything; decisive action from us is needed if the future God intends for our world is to come about.

In that sense, as Jesus remarks in his comment on the parable, the children of light have something to learn from the children of this world. In contemporary terms we could say that the church has something to learn from the world of business. The church is not a business, but it certainly needs to keep a close watch on best practice in the business world, whether that relates to sound planning procedures, to the efficient use of resources or to the proper care and training of the workforce.

As disciples of Jesus, we are both children of this world and children of light. We live in the midst of the secular world and we can learn from how that world operates. Yet we are called to live in that world as those who have been enlightened by the gospel of Christ, to allow the light of the gospel to shape the way that we live in the world. We are to bring the values of God's kingdom to bear on the world where we live and work.

God's values and God's vision will often come into conflict with how our world tends to operate. According to today's readings, God's vision for our world requires money to be used in the service of others, especially of those who are most vulnerable. The prophet Amos rails against those who make money by undermining the well being of the needy. Jesus calls on us to use money to win the kind of friends who will welcome us into the tents of eternity. The steward used his master's money to gain earthly friends. We are to use money to gain heavenly friends. Elsewhere in the gospel of Luke, Jesus makes clear what this entails. It means using money in the service of those who are in greatest need, and treating earthly riches as a resource given to us in trust by God for the well being of others.

Twenty-Sixth Sunday in Ordinary Time

We appreciate people who notice. To notice is more than just physically seeing; it entails seeing beyond the obvious to what is really there. You might be able to think of a time when you were going through a difficult experience and someone noticed in that sense. Having noticed, they may have gone on to express their awareness in some thoughtful way or other. There are times when we see without noticing. People send us signals that we miss. That may be more the case today than it was in the past. We tend to live life at a faster pace today. We can be so focused on what is ahead that we miss what is on either side of us. We have not the time to notice, to pay attention to what we see. It may not always be a matter of time. We can fail to notice because at some deep level we fear that if we do notice it will make too many demands on us. We protect ourselves by not noticing. When we ask people 'How are you?' part of us probably hopes that they will not tell us.

The story that Jesus told in today's gospel reading is about the failure to notice. The rich man failed to notice Lazarus at his gate. He must have seen Lazarus almost every day at his gate, but he saw him without noticing him. The gospel suggests that the rich man failed to notice, not because he was too busy or in too much of a hurry, but because he was too self-absorbed. In the words of last Sunday's gospel reading, he was the servant of his wealth; he was so immersed in his own lifestyle that he had lost the ability to notice the likes of Lazarus at his gate. The gospel reading also suggests that his lifestyle so absorbed him that he had ceased to notice God or God's call. If he had been attentive to God he would have recognised that God was calling out to him through the wretched man who sat at his gate. The rich man had five brothers who were somewhat like himself. They too were self-absorbed, immersed in their own comfortable world; they too failed to notice what God was saying to them through Moses and the prophets; they too were not hearing God's call to them though the sufferings of fellow human beings.

The story Jesus told was not one about two groups of people or two classes of people, but about two individuals. Many of the stories Jesus told were about individual human beings. God comes to us in the individual who crosses our path. The Lord calls out to us through the concrete human being with whom we come face to face. We are called to notice not just in some global, general way, but in a very particular way. We are to notice the particular individual who stands before us at any particular time. We are to respond to the concrete person in accordance with how God has spoken to us through Moses and the prophets, in the words of the gospel reading. As followers of Christ, we are to respond to that concrete person in accordance with how God has spoken to us through his Son. Jesus has told us that when another human being stands before us in need, he himself is standing before us. 'I was hungry and you gave me food, I was thirsty and you gave me drink, I was a stranger and you welcomed me.' Jesus identifies himself there not with a class of people but with the individual person who comes before us, who engages us in conversation, who looks towards us, who cries out to us.

When two people meet, it can sometimes be difficult to know who the needy one really is. In the story that Jesus told, at one level it is obvious that Lazarus is the needy one. Yet, in reality, the rich man was in greater need. In spite of Lazarus' misery, his future was secure. For all the rich man's good fortune, his future was anything but secure. There is a sense in which the rich man needed Lazarus more than Lazarus needed him. Lazarus was assured of salvation, whereas the rich man's path to salvation was through Lazarus. It was in responding to Lazarus that the rich man would have made it to Abraham's bosom. When someone who appears to be in much greater need than me crosses my path, I may be the really needy one and that person may be my path to salvation. It is in noticing that person and responding that I can become the person the Lord is calling me to be.

Twenty-Seventh Sunday in Ordinary Time

Most of us will hit a crisis in our lives sooner or later. It might have to do with the state of our health or with the loss of a loved one or with an important relationship in our lives breaking down. Times of crisis can affect our relationship with God. In such times we easily identify with the words of the prophet Habakkuk in today's first reading: 'How long, Lord, am I to cry for help while you will not listen; to cry "Oppression" in your ear and you will not save?' This is the cry of the believer who has serious questions to ask of God, and whose relationship with God is strained, to say the least.

I find the outburst of Habakkuk in today's reading rather reassuring. It reminds us that our relationship with God can pass through a great variety of phases. In that sense it is like our closest human relationships. Most of the time we relate in a very positive way to those closest to us, but there will be times when those relationships are marked by anger, disappointment, confusion. The presence of these emotions is not necessarily a sign that the relationship is in serious trouble; it is simply a sign that the relationship is human. Habakkuk's questions to God reveal his anger, disappointment and confusion with God. Yet, he was very much a believer. When we find those same emotions entering our relationship with God, it is not necessarily a sign that our faith is weakening.

We can make the mistake of thinking that faith is always a joyful and satisfying experience and then, when it is not so, to imagine that our faith is diminishing. The disciples in today's gospel reading seem to be concerned about how much faith they had. They turned to Jesus and asked for more faith, 'Increase our faith.' However, Jesus did not respond to their request as they might have expected. He did not say to them, 'Yes, your faith is weak, I will give you more.' Instead he stressed to them the power of a faith that is no bigger than a mustard seed, the smallest of all the seeds. In other words, when it comes to faith, the issue is not one of quantity. Jesus suggests that even the tiniest level of faith is enough for God. God can touch our lives through even the tiniest of openings that we make.

The prayer of the disciples in today's gospel reading is one we find easy to identify with. We can sometimes feel vaguely dissatisfied about our faith, and wonder about the state of our relationship with God. We might even describe ourselves as hanging on by a thread. If Jesus takes mustard seeds seriously, he probably takes threads seriously too. The thread may be all that the Lord needs to continue relating to us. At the end of the day, faith as small as a mustard seed is all that God needs.

The parable that Jesus speaks in today's gospel reading suggests that what really matters in our relationship with God is that we hang on in there. The setting of the story is drawn from the culture in which Jesus lived. The servant in the story did what was asked of him; he dutifully kept to his routine day after day. He embodies faithfulness and reliability. In our relationship with God, we are simply called to be faithful, to stay the course, even when our faith seems no bigger that a mustard seed. At times we may feel that God is very distant from us. We may consider that our religious practice has become something of a routine with little excitement; we may wonder if we are just going through the motions. We may even suspect that we are losing faith. The parable assures us that God values our faithful service, even when we are tempted to make light of it. God will keep us faithful, if we ask him to do so. In that sense, faith is more God's doing than ours. Faith is always God's gift to us, and it is given to all who desire it, no matter how small that desire may appear to us. A desire the size of a mustard seed is all God needs to bestow his gifts.

Today we are invited to treasure the gift of faith that God has given us, even if it appears to us to be no bigger than a mustard seed. As Paul reminds Timothy in today's second reading: 'You have been trusted to look after something precious.' We will need the support of other believers if we are to be faithful. We are very dependant on each other's mustard seed of faith.

Twenty-Eighth Sunday in Ordinary Time

If you go into any good stationary shop today you will find a great range of cards. Among the range you will certainly find a selection of thank-you cards. I am always threatening to buy a bundle of them so as to have them to hand. However, when I really need one, I more often than not discover that I have run out of them.

Some people are very good at sending thank-you cards. Perhaps the majority of us are not good at saying 'thank you'. My father had a number of sayings that he came out with from time to time, and one of them was, 'eaten bread is soon forgotten'. He was referring to how easy it can be to take things for granted – and, indeed, to take people for granted. There is something about the sense of being taken for granted – about ingratitude – that can hurt us deeply. It can drain us of energy; we can find ourselves saying, 'Why bother?' I suppose if we were saints, lack of appreciation from others would not impact on us in any significant way. In contrast, an expression of gratitude is very life-giving. Gratitude invariably affirms and empowers us. If we are prone to doubting ourselves, it can reassure us and encourage us to keep going.

Gratitude is the response to being gifted. If we do a day's work and get paid at the end of it, we would not send a thank you card to the boss. Our salary is not a gift; it is a right; we have worked for it. Gratitude comes into play when we receive a gift, when we are graced in some way. In reality, a great deal of what we really value in life is gift, coming to us from beyond ourselves – whether it is a beautiful sunset or wonderful music or, indeed, the people that really matter to us. The presence of such people in our lives is probably not the result of hard work and effort. Yes, keeping a significant relationship alive once it has begun can be hard work, but the origin of the relationship is invariably more in the nature of gift received than reward worked for. Because so much in life is gift, there is great scope for gratitude. A lack of gratitude in our lives can indicate our failure to appreciate just how much we have been gifted, just how much of what we really value has been received rather than earned.

As believers we recognise that all the gifts of life have their ultimate origin in God, the great giver. St James in his letter puts it well when he says: 'Every good gift is from above, coming down from the Father of lights.' As believers, when we recognise that we have been graced by someone, our gratitude to that person becomes gratitude to God, whom we recognise as the ultimate source of all grace. That is what distinguished the one leper from the other nine in the gospel reading. All had been graced by Jesus. The illness that kept them isolated from all except other lepers had been taken away. Only one of them recognized that the ultimate source of this wonderful grace was God. The gospel reading tells us that, finding himself cured, he turned back praising God at the top of his voice. He threw himself at the feet of Jesus, thanking him, because he recognised that God had worked through Jesus to cure him. The real object of the leper's thanks was not so much Jesus, but God present in Jesus. This is what Jesus recognised. Jesus did not say, 'No one has come back to thank me except this foreigner', but, rather, 'No one has come back to praise God except this foreigner.' What distinguished this leper from the other nine was that he recognised his healing as a gift, and he further recognised God as the source of this gift. This is the vision of faith. 'Your faith has saved you,' Jesus said to him.

We are called to grow into that same vision of faith, exemplified by that Samaritan leper. It is good to take time to name the ways we have been graced through life, to recognise God as the source of all these gifts, and to lift up our hearts in praise and thanksgiving to God. Our presence at Mass is a wonderful opportunity to do just that. The word 'Eucharist' comes from the Greek word for 'thanksgiving'. At Mass we enter into Jesus' own prayer of praise and thanksgiving to God. We are caught up into the prayer of the risen Lord. Through him, with him and in him, we return thanks to God for all we receive.

Twenty-Ninth Sunday in Ordinary Time

We live in an age where what is instant is greatly valued. In the past, for example, food took a long time to prepare and to cook. Today, we can buy a product, put it in the microwave, and we have a hot meal with minimal labour and expenditure of time. Journeys that in the past took months, now take hours. With emailing, messages that once took days to go from one place to another now take seconds. Speed is a phenomenon of our time. Much of this is to be welcomed. A huge range of possibilities are now open to us that an earlier generation could not even have imagined possible.

Yet, for all the speed of much of modern life, we know that the pace of some things has not changed. Oak trees do not grow much quicker today than they did hundreds of years ago. The earth's orbit around the sun has not quickened over millions of years. The time it takes to build true friendships with people has not significantly changed. The forming of good relationships continues to take time and patience; it is characterised by both progress and set-backs; ground that is lost often has to be re-gained. The quality of perseverance is needed in human relationships, the willingness to work through difficulties, perhaps with help from others. Perseverance is a quality that comes into play in those areas of life that are not amenable to instant solution.

The parable that Jesus speaks in the gospel reading this morning suggests that we will need that quality of perseverance or persistence in our relationship with God. Jesus tells a story of a powerful man, a judge, and a powerless woman, a widow. The widow knew that she had justice on her side, and it was her passion for justice that gave her the quality of persistence. She kept coming to the judge looking for justice, refusing to take 'no' for an answer. Even though she was powerless, her persistence made her powerful. The power of her persistence wore down the powerful judge and she eventually received the justice she was entitled to. Jesus presents this widow as a model of persistent faith. It is not that God is like the unjust judge in the parable. On the contrary, God's passion for justice is greater than our own. It is rather that we will need something of her persistent faith if God's justice is to become a reality in our midst. The widow's efforts did not meet with instant success; her pleas did not receive an instant answer. Yet, she persevered and her persistence brought about what God wanted to happen.

When we pray in the 'Our Father' 'thy kingdom come', we are really praying, 'thy justice come'. God's kingdom comes whenever human beings relate to each other justly and lovingly. God's kingdom is present when the vulnerable are given protection, when those unjustly treated are given justice, and when those with power use it justly and selflessly. We are only too well aware today that God's kingdom has not fully come. The justice that God passionately desires for our world is not yet a reality among us. We need to keep on praying 'thy kingdom come' and not lose heart. Our persevering prayer for the coming of God's kingdom will only be a genuine prayer if it is lived out in some way. We need both to pray and to work with perseverance for the coming of God's kingdom. The widow in the parable did more than just utter words; the parable tells us that she kept on coming to the judge. She walked from where she lived to where the judge lived in order to make her request, and she did that repeatedly. That took time and energy. Our prayer for the coming of God's kingdom, if it is really coming from our heart, will also take us on a journey. It will inspire us to keep on doing whatever we can to ensure that God's justice is a reality in our neighbourhood, in our society, in our world. At the end of the parable, Jesus asks the question, 'When the Son of Man comes, will he find any faith on earth?' That question is addressed to all of us. Will the persistent prayer and action of the widow for God's justice be evident among us?

There are many contemporary examples of the persistent prayer of the widow in today's world, people whose passion for justice empowers them to persist in the face of official stone walling and resistance. When the seemingly powerless are filled with God's passion for justice they become powerful, like the widow in the gospel reading. Today we might pray for something of her passionate faith in our own lives.

Thirtieth Sunday in Ordinary Time

We live in a very competitive age. We can all appreciate the value of good competition. Because of it, we can all travel by air much more cheaply than we could have done in the past. We like to be able to compare prices and to have the freedom to take the cheapest option. There can be a down side to the competitive spirit also. In the world of work and business there is often a lot of pressure on people to work out of the mentality of the league table. We can be made to feel that we should be rising higher and higher in the table. This leads us to see ourselves in relation to others. Am I doing better or worse than my competitors? Am I higher or lower in the table than others? This tendency to look at everything through the lens of the league table is not always appropriate. Many people in the world of education, for example, are very unhappy with the notion that there should be a league table of schools which would indicate which schools get the best exam results and produce the biggest number of university candidates. They are only too well aware that there is not a level playing field for schools and therefore the notion of a league table is inherently unfair. Some schools face a much bigger challenge than others in virtue of their location and the catchment area from which they draw their pupils. Whereas there can be a great value in competition, in certain areas of life it can undermine other, perhaps more important, values.

One of the two characters in the parable that Jesus speaks in today's gospel reading appears to have a very competitive spirit when it comes to the area of moral living. He considers himself to be much further up the league table than those he refers to as 'the rest of mankind'. He certainly thinks of himself as very far above the tax collector who happens to be in the Temple in Jerusalem with him. In fact, he is likely to have said that he is in a different league all together. He had good reason to think that this was the case. He could point to objective data which clearly supported his contention that he was much further up the ladder connecting heaven to earth than the tax collector was. The parable is not in any way presenting the Pharisee as a figure of fun. The vast majority of his contemporaries would have agreed with his assessment of himself and of the tax collector. This would have been the common sense perspective on both of these men.

Because we have heard it so often, it is difficult to appreciate the shock that the hearers of this parable would have experienced when, having told the story, Jesus then commented on it by saying that the tax collector went home at rights with God, whereas the Pharisee did not. It is easy to imagine his listeners responding with a comment like, 'You can't be serious.' Although what the Pharisee said about himself was correct and right, it could be said that he was right in the wrong way, he was right in a way that made him contemptuous of a fellow human being. Jesus is declaring here that, when the price to be paid for our being in the right is contempt for others, our position becomes fatally undermined in the eyes of God. Indeed, the parable strongly suggests that, when it comes to the question of how we stand with God, comparing ourselves with others is a useless exercise, because we are almost certain to get it wrong.

The tax collector, for all his flaws and failings, did not get into the business of comparing himself with others in God's presence. He was content to look into his own heart only and he made no claim to know the hearts of others. It took him all his time to face the darkness in his own life, without speculating on what forms of darkness might be in the lives of others. His prayer, 'God, be merciful to me a sinner', was a genuine prayer. It came straight from the depths of his own truth. He could face the disturbing truth of his life because, in his heart of hearts, he believed that God's mercy was greater than his own sin, and he trusted that God always receives those who pray out of the awareness of their own poverty. The difference between the Pharisee and the tax collector came down to the issue of trust. The Pharisee trusted in himself; the tax collector trusted in God. The Pharisee built his house on sand, the tax collector on rock.

Thirty-First Sunday in Ordinary Time

We can probably all think of certain initiatives we took in the past that turned out to be very significant both for ourselves and for others. There is a sense in which it is true to say that we can make things happen. There are initiatives that only I can take and if I do not take them something worthwhile that would have come from such initiatives will simply not happen. This holds true in all areas of our lives, including our relationship with the Lord. There are initiatives we can take to deepen that relationship and to live our baptism more fully. There are other initiatives we could take that would weaken that relationship and undermine our living of our faith. Opportunities come our way to grow in our relationship with the Lord and there are consequences to taking and to not taking those opportunities.

The figure of Zacchaeus in today's gospel reading is an example of someone who took the initiative to seize an opportunity when it came his way. Here was a person whose public profile was very negative. Because of his occupation as a tax collector, people identified him as a 'sinner'. He was presumed to be a cheat, who had acquired his wealth by exploiting his own people. As a 'sinner' it was believed that he did not have any relationship with God but, rather, was outside the scope of God's concern. Yet, in labelling him a 'sinner', people had gravely misjudged and underestimated him. Yes, he was far from perfect, but there was within him what St Paul calls, in today's second reading, 'desires for goodness'. He was not content with the place where he found himself. There was a restlessness in him, a longing for something more.

This restlessness led him to take an initiative when an opportunity arose. He had heard about Jesus' reputation as a man of God, and when Jesus was passing through Jericho, Zacchaeus ran ahead and climbed a sycamore tree to see him. That action of running and climbing bespeaks a strong desire to make contact with goodness, to deepen his relationship with God. Zacchaeus' initiative placed him within eye contact of Jesus. In response to Zacchaeus' initiative, Jesus took an initiative of his own, calling Zacchaeus by name and declaring to him, 'I must stay at your house, today.' Jesus related to him, not as a sinner to be avoided, but as someone who had a deep desire for goodness. Jesus engaged with his desire, rather than with his reputation. He went on to publicly declare that Zacchaeus was more than a sinner; he was as much a son of Abraham as anyone else was. He may have been considered an outsider by most people, but to God he was an insider because his heart was in the right place.

The view that most people had of Zacchaeus did not do him justice, whereas Jesus' vision of him was much more generous and truer to the reality of his life. The Lord's vision of us is always more generous than the view that we tend to have of ourselves and of others. The first reading today puts it well: 'You love all that exists; you hold nothing of what you have made in abhorrence.' The Lord recognises the desires for goodness that are deeply embedded in us, and he engages with those desires and responds to them whenever we give expression to them. Whatever initiative we might take in keeping with those desires will be matched by an even greater initiative from the Lord towards us. He alone can fulfil our desires for goodness, and if we are faithful to those desires, he will not fail us. If Zacchaeus had taken the perception that other people had of him at face value, he would never have climbed that tree. We need to be true to what is best within us, even when that is not recognised by others.

Our being true to our desires for goodness can lead us to do something extravagant and unconventional. Climbing a tree would have been considered an unconventional action for a man of the professional stature of Zacchaeus. There are times when we too might need to go out on a limb if we are to meet the Lord for whom our hearts are restless. In the culture in which we live, taking initiatives to deepen our relationship with the Lord can be regarded as somewhat odd and eccentric. There can be all kinds of subtle pressures on us to conform to what is considered acceptable. The Lord went out on a limb for us, laying down his life on a cross. Sometimes, he will ask us to go out on a limb for him.

Thirty-Second Sunday in Ordinary Time

November is a month when the church invites us to remember those who have died. Not all our memories are happy ones. Some memories can be painful. Looking back is not always easy. Yet, we all have happy memories, good memories, of people, now dead, who enriched our lives. November is a month to remember with affection all those past friendships and relationships that have graced and blessed us.

In remembering such people, in calling them to mind, we allow them to continue to influence us and engage with us. Although they have died, we believe that their life has changed, not ended. They continue to be present to us in a different way. In remembering them, we open ourselves up to their presence. For us as Christians, memory is not so much a journey back into the past where someone once was. It is more a becoming aware of someone who remains present to us, even if not in a visible way. We believe in the communion of saints, in that deep bond between those of us who are still on our pilgrim way and those who have come to the end of their earthly journey. Whenever we remember those who have died, we allow ourselves to become conscious of that deep bond between them and us. Memory in that sense is like a gate that opens us up to those who continue to be with us in Christ.

There are some who believe that for those who have died, life is indeed ended not changed. The Sadducees who approach Jesus in today's gospel reading were of that view. They attempt to show the absurdity of life after death by presenting Jesus with a scenario that they consider makes nonsense of that belief. In reply, Jesus states that life beyond death will be qualitatively different to life before death, and that the scenario they present simply does not apply in this qualitatively different life. Jesus is saying to them that for those who have died, life has changed. It has not ended; neither does it remain the same. Of course, we would love to know in more detail what this change of life will consist in. On the basis of what Jesus says in today's gospel reading, and of what is said in the rest of the New Testament, we do know that this changed life will involve a deeper relationship with God. As today's responsorial psalm puts it, 'I shall see your face, and be filled with the sight of your glory.' If God is the source of life, a deeper relationship with God can only make us more alive.

Prayer is attentiveness to God, the God of the living, not of the dead, as Jesus says in today's gospel reading. Memory is attentiveness to those who are alive in God. When we remember our departed loved ones, we become attuned again to those for whom life has changed, not ended. Our memory of our departed loved ones can be triggered in a whole variety of ways. It might be a photograph or a fragrance or a piece of music or a particular place. Many people find that their loved ones come to mind in a religious setting, at prayer in a church, at Mass, when gathered with other believers to worship. If we believe that our departed loved ones have been brought into a deeper relationship with God, it is not surprising that when we become more attuned to God's presence we also become more aware of them. We long for a fuller communion with our departed loves ones. That longing will only be satisfied when we too will have reached the end of our earthly pilgrimage.

One of the ways we give expression to our present communion with our departed loved ones is by praying for them. The church encourages us to do this, particularly in the month of November. Prayer for each other is at the heart of our Christian life. In today's second reading we find Paul praying for the believers in Thessalonica. In praying for the members of the church in Thessalonica, Paul also calls on them to pray for him. 'Pray for us,' he says, 'pray that the Lord's message may spread quickly.' Paul appreciated that he needed to pray for others and that he needed others to pray for him. We all need to pray for each other. Our prayer for those who are significant for us does not cease when they pass from this world, and neither does their prayer for us. When we pray for our loved ones who have died, we are really asking that the Lord would bring to completion the good work that he began in them at their baptism.

Thirty-Third Sunday in Ordinary Time

I once heard an interview with a captain from the Salvation Army who works full time in one of the church's shelters for homeless people. At one point the interviewer asked him if he had ever had serious doubts about his faith. He answered that the tragic events in the small North Ossetian town of Beslan some years ago was a real challenge to his faith. The killing of so many children, some of whom were shot in the back as they ran away, rocked his faith. Yet, his faith survived that troubling experience. It was clear from the interview that he has remained a man of deep faith, a faith that bears fruit in a life of service.

Many of us, I am sure, could point to some experience that really put our faith to the test. It will often be a very personal event that does not make the news or attract international attention. Our faith can take a battering when we are exposed to the darker side of life, when we are brought face to face with some very obvious expression of evil. We can find ourselves struggling to make sense of what we are experiencing. A relationship with God does not of itself protect us from the darker side of life. Our faith in the Lord has to be strong enough to endure the experience of evil and suffering. To believe in God is to look the darkness in the face with hope, and even with love.

In the gospel reading we just heard, Jesus very deliberately talks to his disciples about the darkness that will come their way. When they comment on the beautiful building that was the Temple in Jerusalem, he tells them bluntly that one day it will all be destroyed. The Temple was the symbol of God's presence for the Jews. Yet, Jesus could see it was doomed. The fall of the Temple is but one element of a very dark scene that Jesus describes – a scene that includes natural disasters, terrible wars, and the persecution of his own followers. It would have been much easier for the disciples to have gone on admiring the beauty of the Temple than to have had to listen to such a dark prediction. Jesus, however, was alert to the darker side of life at that time, because he was on the point of having to face into his own very personal experience of darkness. The hour of his passion and death was imminent.

Jesus clearly wanted his disciples to have a faith that was robust enough to deal with the darkness of evil and suffering. He wants all of us to have a faith that endures. In 'your endurance will win you your lives', he says in that reading. An enduring faith is a faith that never losses hope in God's power to bring good out of evil, new life out of death. An enduring faith is ready to hope against hope. As Christians, our approach to life is shaped by the events of Easter Sunday. The evil and sin that was the hill of Calvary was not the last word. God worked powerfully through that dark experience for the healing and the salvation of all, including the salvation of those who brought that darkness about. When the darkness of sin and evil seems to be at its most powerful, we are called to have a faith that endures. Such endurance is not just the result of will power on our part. It is the Lord who keeps us faithful. In the gospel reading Jesus tells his disciples that he himself will give them the eloquence and the wisdom they need when their faith is tested. When our own faith is put to the test, we will not be standing alone.

The final failure of the Christian is to succumb to a sense of hopelessness and helplessness in the face of darkness and, as a result, to throw in the towel, to give up on the Lord's good work. In the garden of Gethsemane, Jesus himself was tempted to retreat before the darkness that awaited him. Yet, his prayer gave him the strength to keep going. Today more than ever, we who have been baptised into the Lord's body also need to stay the course. As today's gospel reading puts it, 'this is your opportunity to bear witness'. The Lord calls on us to keep faithful, bearing witness to him by what we say and do, in our homes, in our places of work, in our parish, in our society. We will need each other's example if we are to be faithful to this call. The endurance of any one of us is an inspiration to us all.

Feast of Christ the King

In today's gospel reading, one of the two men who were crucified with Jesus said of him: 'This man has done nothing wrong.'
In saying this of Jesus, he was making a very clear distinction between Jesus, on the one hand, and himself and his fellow criminal, on the other. With reference to himself and his fellow criminal, he said: 'In our case, we deserved it; we are paying for what
we did.' He thereby acknowledges that the same fate, in this
case crucifixion, can befall the innocent and the guilty alike. In
other words, how people die often bears no relationship to how
they have lived. The treatment Jesus received in his death bore
no relationship to the way he treated others in the course of his
life. This can be true of many people in our own time as well.

Those who crucified Jesus did not recognise his goodness. As
today's gospel shows, they mocked and jeered him; they
shamed and humiliated him. The title over the cross, 'Jesus of
Nazareth, king of the Jews,' was put there as a joke. Yet, in the
midst of all this blindness and mockery, there were a couple of
people who saw more deeply than most, who recognised that
this broken man was indeed someone special. The Roman
centurion recognised Jesus' special relationship with God, and a
man at the opposite end of the spectrum to the centurion, one of
the two crucified criminals, recognised that there was something regal about Jesus, that he was indeed a king, that he had a
kingdom, although one that was not of this world. The prayer of
this man has become the prayer of many Christians throughout
the generations: 'Remember me when you come into your kingdom.' The response of Jesus to this man has also spoken to
Christians down the generations: 'I promise you, today you will
be with me in Paradise.' Jesus was accompanied into Paradise
by one whom the world considered damned.

This criminal, this waster as many would have seen him, was
much more perceptive than the religious leaders of the day. He
recognised the truth in the mockery of others. Jesus was indeed
a king, who had come to proclaim the kingdom of God. This
man saw clearly that here was a king who embodied the merciful and loving rule of God, to whom one could turn in confidence out of one's misery and sinfulness. This man's way of see-

ing showed that, in a sense, he already belonged to the kingdom of God. His seeing was a graced seeing. He saw with the eyes of God; he was open to God's way of seeing. He recognised the goodness that so many others were blind to. Many others demonised Jesus' goodness, declaring that he healed people by the power of Satan.

Today's feast of Christ the King invites us to identify with the one person in today's gospel reading whose vision was pure and undefiled. He saw himself and Jesus clearly. I think most of us are aware just how easily our vision can become distorted. Our view of others can be very restricted at times. We can focus on one small element in their make-up and be blind to much more significant elements. Our restricted way of seeing another can be most in evidence when the other person is different from us in some significant way, when they are not one of us, so to speak.

The good thief, as he is often called, recognised the presence of God's kingdom in the crucified Jesus. Even in the midst of a situation that was steeped in darkness, he saw the signs of God's kingdom. We too are called to recognise the signs of God's kingdom in our own midst, especially in the lives of those where we might not expect to find them. The evil and misery in the world can sometimes blind us to the signs of the kingdom. Yet, these signs are there for those who have eyes to see. God's kingdom is present whenever someone who asks to be remembered is responded to with a word of comfort and hope. God's kingdom is present whenever mercy is shown to those who need it, whenever those who are struggling reach out to support fellow strugglers, whenever justice is done for those who have been deprived of it. God's kingdom is present whenever we remain faithful to the call of the gospel, whenever we hold to gospel values, even in situations where such values are ridiculed.

God's kingdom comes whenever God's will is done on earth as it is in heaven. On this feast of Christ the King, we commit ourselves again to doing God's will as Jesus reveals it, so that the signs of God's kingdom may be more plentiful among us.

Saint Patrick

In celebrating the feast of St Patrick, we are celebrating the roots of our Christian faith on this island. We remember him as the great preacher of the gospel in our land. He lit a flame that has remained lighting for close on sixteen hundred years. We are very fortunate that two of Patrick's own writings have been preserved, his *Confessions* and a letter he wrote to the soldiers of a chieftain named Coroticus. Through these writings the voice of Patrick continues to be heard among us. It is his *Confessions* that give us the fascinating story of his life.

Patrick was born a citizen of Roman Britain. His father was a town councillor, part of the Roman administration in southern Britain, who owned a country residence with male and female servants. Patrick came from a Christian family. His father was a priest and his grandfather a deacon. Yet, as a youth, Patrick's faith was lukewarm, to say the least. Looking back on his youth many years later, he writes in his *Confessions*: 'We had turned away from God; we did not keep his commandments.' We can imagine that he must have been a disappointment to his family.

Then at the tender age of sixteen, his comfortable world came crashing down around him. Writing in his *Confessions*, he says: 'I was taken captive as a youth, a mere child ... I was taken into captivity in Ireland with many thousands of people.' At a vulnerable and impressionable age, he was wrenched from the family that loved him. He was taken from his home, his friends, his culture, and he found himself a slave in a foreign land. An experience like that could destroy a young man. Yet, Patrick tells us that in his harsh exile, he had a powerful experience of God's presence. When everything had been taken from him, he found God or, rather, God found him. He writes in his *Confessions* about 'the great benefits that the Lord saw fit to confer on me in my captivity'. He uses a powerful image to describe this great spiritual reawakening: 'Before I was humbled, I was like a stone lying in the deep mud. Then he who is mighty came and in his mercy he not only pulled me out but lifted me up and placed me at the very top of the wall.' In the wilderness of his exile, his faith came alive.

He goes on to tell us in his *Confessions* that six years after first coming to Ireland as a slave, at the age of twenty two, he managed to escape from his captivity. He was taken on board a boat, and eventually made his way back to Roman Britain. What a home coming that must have been for his parents. They thought he was dead, and here he was alive. Patrick states that 'They earnestly begged me that I should never leave them.'

Some years later, Patrick tells us, he had a vision of a man who appeared to have come from Ireland with a large number of letters. In his vision, Patrick took one of these letters in his hands, and as he began to read it he heard a crowd shout with one voice: 'We ask you, boy, come and walk once more among us.' That vision touched him deeply. He did not come back to Ireland immediately. He first pursued higher studies in preparation for the priesthood, probably in Roman Gaul. He came to Ireland initially as a priest and, having established himself as a missionary, he was appointed bishop. He writes in his *Confessions*: 'I came to the Irish heathen to preach the good news.' It is extraordinary that Patrick was prepared to endure voluntary exile to bring the gospel to a people among whom he had experienced captivity. He brought the precious gift of his faith to those who had taken away his freedom many years earlier. I am reminded of a line in one of Paul's letters: 'Do not be overcome by evil, but overcome evil with good.'

Patrick's story can still speak to us over the centuries. The darkest moment in his life proved to be life-giving, both for himself and for the people in the land of his captivity. We are all familiar with dark moments in our own lives. In ways we might never suspect at the time, such experiences can turn out to be life-giving for ourselves and for others. God can work powerfully in and through us in those dark times. Patrick's feast day invites us to trust that God can turn even our darkest experiences to good and can bring unexpected new life out of our losses. That can be true both of us as individuals and of us as a community of believers, a church.

Feast of the Assumption

We have all experienced, to some degree, the value of visitation, of visiting others or being visited by them. We can all think of occasions when we went on a journey to visit friends or family members. If we were well received and welcomed, the visit more than likely did us good. We came away the better for the visit and, perhaps, we extended an invitation to those we visited to visit us in return. Making a visit or receiving a visit has the potential to deepen the bond between the visitor and the one visited.

In today's gospel reading we hear the story of Mary's visit to Elizabeth. Luke describes a visit that left the visitor and the one visited greatly blessed. As a result of Mary's visit Elizabeth was filled with the Holy Spirit, and because of the way Mary's visit was received by Elizabeth, Mary herself was filled with the spirit of prayer and praise, the Holy Spirit. Luke describes a visit that was truly life-giving for both Mary and Elizabeth.

Elizabeth addresses Mary as 'the mother of my Lord'. She recognised that in welcoming Mary she was welcoming the Lord whom Mary was carrying. Elizabeth was aware that the Lord was visiting her through Mary, and so she declared Mary blessed. That is why we honour Mary too. We recognise that it was through her that the Lord visited us. Later on in Luke's gospel the crowds will say of the adult Jesus: 'A great prophet has arisen among us and God has visited his people.' The really significant visitation is God's visiting us in the person of Jesus, and it was through Mary that this visitation happened. It was through this woman of Nazareth that the Lord visited his people and having visited them remained with them, until the end of time. We honour Mary because she was the gate through whom the Lord came to visit us. That is why, as she sings in her Magnificat, all generations have called her blessed.

As the gate though whom the Lord first came to us, Mary has a unique relationship with the Lord and, in virtue of that unique relationship, she shares uniquely in his risen and glorious life. That is what we celebrate today on this feast of the Assumption. We celebrate Mary's complete sharing in her Son's triumph over death. In the words of Paul, in the second reading, she has been brought to life in Christ. What Mary has become, we hope to be. The great thing that God has done for Mary is a pointer to the great thing that God wants to do for all of us.

Unlike Mary, we are still on the way, 'our pilgrim way', as today's Preface puts it. Mary's life puts before us how we might travel that pilgrim way. Like her, we are called to be channels of the Lord's visitation to others. As Mary brought the Lord to Elizabeth and to all of us, we are called to bring the Lord to each other, so that those who meet us might come to say, 'The Lord has visited his people.' This is the best way to honour Mary. In honouring Mary in this way, we can be assured that, at the end of our pilgrim way, the Lord will honour us as he honoured her, and will do the same great things for us that he has done for her.

Feast of the Immaculate Conception

Mary's freedom from sin was widely proclaimed in the early church. However, the formal declaration of Mary's freedom from sin was made by Pius IX in 1854 when he declared that Mary 'from the first moment of her conception was preserved from all stain of sin, by the singular grace and privilege of God and by the merits of Jesus Christ, the Saviour of the world'.

The greeting of Gabriel to Mary in this morning's gospel, 'Hail, full of grace', captures the meaning of today's feast. Mary is full of God's gracious love. If the essence of sin is turning away from God, Mary is totally turned towards God, completely open to God's love and to God's presence. Her openness is captured in her final words in today's gospel reading: 'I am the handmaid of the Lord. Let what you have said be done to me.'

We live in a world where at times sin and evil seem to reign supreme. The first reading presents the human tendency to hide from God and to go against what God asks of us. The portrayal of Adam in the first reading stands in contrast to the portrayal of Mary in the gospel. Most of us find ourselves somewhere in between both. We are aware of our tendency to hide from God and to do our own thing, like Adam, and yet we sense a call to turn towards God and to open ourselves completely to God's presence, like Mary. Paul refers to this call in today's second reading, when he tells us that God has chosen us in Christ to be holy and spotless and to live through love in God's presence.

Today we celebrate the good news that at least one human being, Mary, has responded fully to that call of God. As we strive to answer that same call, we look to Mary for inspiration and for help. We ask her to pray for us, sinners, now and at the hour of our death, so that God's grace and love that embraced Mary from the first moment of her existence would also touch our lives.

While today's feast celebrates Mary's unique sinlessness, it should not detract from her humanity. Her holiness was lived amidst the struggles and sorrows of this world. Her son was a sign of contradiction, a sword pierced her own soul; she often puzzled over the words and actions of her son, and she suffered the unique agony of a parent who sees an offspring die. She knew the darker side of life and, yet, in the midst of it all, she remained completely open to God and to God's will for her life. Her humanity makes her holiness in some way accessible to us.

What was said to Mary in today's gospel reading is said to all of us: 'The Lord is with you.' Mary was completely open to the Lord's presence to her. The season of Advent calls on us to be as open to the Lord's presence as Mary was, to be as responsive to his call as she was.

Feast of All Saints

I heard a story of a priest who went into a classroom in the local primary school and asked the children who the saints were. One of them, thinking of the stained glass window in her church, said that a saint was someone who let the light in. She said more than she realised. Saints are those who allow the light of Christ's presence to shine through them.

Today we remember those referred to in the first reading today as that 'huge number, impossible to count, of people from every nation, race, tribe and language' through whose lives the light of Christ's love streamed into our world. We will all have known such people. They have lived and continue to live among us. We do not have to go on a long pilgrimage to find them. They are the people whose lives have blessed and graced us in a whole variety of ways. When we think of them, we thank God for them. When we have been in their company, we feel the better for it. They somehow brought out the best in us and helped us to become all that God was calling us to be.

In today's gospel reading, Jesus paints a portrait of what it means to be a disciple of his, what someone who lets his light in looks like. Fundamentally, this is Jesus' own self-portrait. There is a sense in which he alone fully fits the portrayal he puts before us. Yet, this is also the person we are all called to be. We can easily think of the beatitudes as describing a variety of types of people – the poor in spirit, the gentle etc. Jesus is really putting before us one type, which can be looked at from various perspectives, like a diamond that appears differently as you look at it from a variety of angles. The elements in Jesus' portrait are of a piece. It is only the poor in spirit, those who acknowledge their dependence on God for everything, who can be true peacemakers. It is only the gentle, those who do not insist on their own way to the detriment of God's way, who can hunger and thirst for what is right, for what corresponds to God's desire for the world. It is only the pure in heart, those who are single-minded in their focus on God and on what God wants, who can be merciful as God is merciful. In speaking the beatitudes, Jesus calls on us to identify with the person he portrays. He wants us to come away from them saying to ourselves, 'This is the person I want to be. This is the life I want to live. Here are shoes that are worth stepping into.'

Today's feast is an opportunity both to give thanks for all those people in our own lives who embodied the beatitudes for us, and to renew our own desire to become the person the Lord portrays. The Lord does not play games with us. He is not holding out something to us that is beyond us, teasing us with what will always be out of reach. He knows that with his help we can grow into the person of the beatitudes. Here is a life that is attainable, a truly human life, a life that is worthy of those who have been made in the image and likeness of God. We appreciate people who take us seriously, who give us a task that corresponds to what we are capable of. The Lord takes us more seriously than any other human being possibly could. It is inconceivable that he could sell us short. He points beyond who we are to who we could be, and he invites us to keep setting out on that journey. As he does so, he promises to travel that journey with us. In calling, he also empowers, as Paul writes at the end of his first letter to the Thessalonians: 'The one who calls you is faithful, and he will do this.'

The life of the beatitudes is not a higher calling that is given to some special caste. We are all called to be saints. St John invites us in the second reading: 'Think of the love that the Father has lavished on us by letting us be called God's children.' God has poured the Spirit of his Son into our hearts crying, 'Abba, Father'. We have been brought into the same relationship with God that Jesus himself has. That is our starting point. Our finishing point is, in the words of that same reading, seeing God as he is. Between such a wonderful starting point and such an unimaginable finishing point, the beatitudes are given to us as a kind of road map.